BYRON BROWNE

DRIVING
SOUTHWEST
TEXAS

On the Road in Big Bend Country

Charleston   London

THE
History
PRESS

Published by The History Press
Charleston, SC 29403
www.historypress.net

All images are courtesy of the author unless otherwise stated.

First published 2011

Manufactured in the United States

ISBN 978.1.60949.072.0

Browne, Byron.
Driving southwest Texas : on the road in Big Bend country / Byron Browne.
p. cm.
Includes bibliographical references and index.
ISBN 978-1-60949-072-0
1. Texas--Guidebooks. 2. Big Bend Region (Tex.)--Guidebooks. 3. Texas, West--Guidebooks. 4. Texas, South--Guidebooks. 5. Automobile travel--Texas--Guidebooks. 6. Historic sites--Texas--Guidebooks. 7. Historic buildings--Texas--Guidebooks. 8. Texas--History, Local. 9. Texas, West--History, Local. 10. Texas, South--History, Local. I. Title.
F384.3.B76 2011
917.64'930464--dc22
2010053832

Notice: The information in this book is true and complete to the best of our knowledge. It is offered without guarantee on the part of the author or The History Press. The author and The History Press disclaim all liability in connection with the use of this book.

For Angie and Taylor. Always.

CONTENTS

Acknowledgements   7
Introduction. Traveling Southwest Texas:
   An Encounter with History and Mythology   9

1. JEFF DAVIS COUNTY   13
*Setting Out * Fort Davis * Don Antonio de Espejo * Historic Fort Davis *
Buffalo Soldiers * Overland Trail Museum * Nick Mersfelder*

2. NORTHEAST BREWSTER COUNTY   34
*Marathon * The Railroad * Musquiz Canyon * Gage Hotel *
Stillwell Store and Ranch * La Linda Bridge*

3. PECOS COUNTY   50
*Ste. Genevieve Winery * Annie Riggs Museum * Paisano Pete * Fort Stockton *
Pecos County Jail * Historic Fort Stockton*

4. NORTHWEST BREWSTER COUNTY   67
*Archives at Sul Ross University * Museum of the Big Bend *
Murphyville/Alpine * H.H. Powe * Kokernot Springs*

5. PRESIDIO COUNTY   86
*Indian Pictograms * Marfa * Presidio County Courthouse *
Marfa Book Company * Paisano Hotel * Marfa/Presidio County Museum *
Poolside Talk * Chinati Foundation * Fort D.A. Russell *
Valentine * Prada Marfa * Marfa Lights*

Contents

6. North-Central Jeff Davis County   112
*McDonald Observatory * Davis Mountains State Park **
*Indian Lodge * Chihuahuan Desert Nature Center*

7. Southwest Brewster County   124
*Terlingua * Quicksilver Mines * Starlight Theatre **
*The Porch * Balmorhea State Park*

8. Southern Brewster County: Big Bend National Park   138

Appendix. Maps   147
Notes   153
Index   157
About the Author   159

ACKNOWLEDGEMENTS

M any thanks are due to those who have made this book a possibility—primarily the Native Americans, perennial inhabitants who were seemingly born from the dust of the ground. These were followed by the early explorers, primarily Spanish, searching for riches for king and country. In turn, the settlers followed, literally, in those footsteps, searching for individual enrichments. Without these extraordinary people, there would be no story, no history to speak of. I am also deeply indebted to those who have written on this subject before, several of whom are quoted here but Clifford Casey and Barry Scobee in particular, not as much for their literary prowess as for the wealth of information they discovered on thousands of blank sheets. Additionally, I want to thank the following for their help and kindnesses: Pat Draheim with the Overland Trail Museum; Ann Marie Nafziger of the Chinati Foundation; Ingólfur Arnarsson; Ilya and Emilia Kabakov; Maria Carrasco; Ring Huggins and all of those on the Porch; Melleta Bell and staff of the Archives at Sul Ross University; Walter Potter; Nan Patton; and Rebecca Johnson with the McDonald Observatory. Finally, an eager and enthusiastic thank-you goes to John and Kate Troesser—*sine quibus non hoc libellum exstet.*

Introduction

Traveling Southwest Texas

An Encounter with History and Mythology

Every journey is its own entity. All journeys are composed of several like components; however, each will acquire its own personality and range of experience: the excitement of the new and trepidation of the unfamiliar, the various stages of planning and preparation, the acquisition of items not typically needed through the course of a regular day and the near subconscious effort to predetermine and imagine those events and adventures that wait at our destinations. The Spanish explorers Alvar Nuñez Cabaza de Vaca and Don Antonio de Espejo, although traveling through the Big Bend regions separated by nearly fifty years, certainly planned for the real and imagined alike. Both men were forever changed by their experiences, and both foresaw the need to record their expeditions and employed official chroniclers (as with Cortez's famous scribe, Bernal Díaz del Castillo).

Certainly, I will not dare compare the weeks that my wife and I spent motoring around southwest Texas with the rigors and very real and hourly dangers experienced by the early explorers and settlers of this region. A serpentine belt snapping in the Big Bend National Park holds a dim candle, if at all, to an attack from enraged Mescalero Apaches. Running out of cigarettes in a moon-locked Fort Davis speaks not at all to sleeping among hungry coyotes and diamondback rattlesnakes. We were employed by no government and under no obligations to deliver any goods or gold (except, maybe, these "goods" for the publisher), and our roads had been cleared and polished generations before by men capable of withstanding a desert's heated temperament.

The automobile is the modern convenience and thrill that allows us to slice and speed through our environments with a rapidity to make even the most ardent explorer envious. In our time, the car has permitted each of us to be adventuresome and curious; it is a crucial component of many travel stories. And for any travel story within the expanse of an area as large as Texas, the automobile is as necessary as water or good directions.

We left a city that is literally bursting at the seams and drove out into what is left of the old frontier. It was just past the city's edges, where the housing developments and strip malls yield to properly squared but shrinking farms and claimed countryside—those border areas where the polis and pastoral compete for space. It is a contest that declared a victor even before the match was begun. However, the juxtaposition (those brackish areas where the struggling dust has yet to settle) produces a wasteland of sorts—quiet, semi-verdant patches of grassland potted with soon-to-be-forgotten indigenous vegetation.

Once past these borders, we came to that area of the state in the far and remote southwest where habitation is posited precariously and where the towns are planted but seem not rooted and are allowed to remain only by nature's benevolence. There is a sense of the temporary out here—where one night's determined storm could swallow a hamlet, and the next morning, Pompeii-like, the place could be gone. It is here that we drive past homes as old as my great-grandfather but supporting façades fading as fast as his health had at the end. It is here that we constantly see the detritus of antique farm equipment, carcasses abandoned in the fields, discarded after failing to bite their metal teeth into ground that allows only scratches. The land here is as stubborn as the people who first chose to inhabit it several thousand years ago.

This is the land we chose to encounter and write about and photograph. As had so many before us, we found the region majestic, sublime and ethereal. There is a reason that this territory has inspired so many pages of text and has filled so many galleries with its images. Every group of people that has traveled through has been branded with the same impression. If, like the hundreds of thousands of head of cattle that have been raised out here, we were all branded with the same insignia, surely that mark would resemble the emblem for eternity: ∞. We would be forever bound to an effort to return again and again. The emotionally magnetic pull of the region is strong, and upon leaving, there is typically a very palpable desire to head right back.

The southwest region of Texas is a relatively small percentage of a large state. However, within that area the state possesses much of what constitutes its character. From the incredible geology to the eye-widening history, the Big Bend region epitomizes all that can be considered Texas.

My wife and I have driven through this area several times. Whether attending the chili cook-off in Terlingua or visiting Jean-Michel Duforat at the Ste. Genevieve winery, we have always enthusiastically looked forward to each and every trip. This one was no different. And because of this book, maybe this time we were more attentive to our surroundings than usual. We spent more time with each objective, tried to understand and enjoy each item just a little more than we would have ordinarily.

For ourselves, at least, I think we succeeded in coming home better educated and more involved with the region. However, I know that we missed or overlooked many places. I know some will wonder why some areas received attention while others did not. The answer is, probably obviously, that there is simply an enormous amount of stuff out here to see and experience. This region of the country was occupied and making history well before any of our ancestors arrived, and the relics and stories that have been left behind are varied and many. It would have been overwhelming to try and incorporate all of this territory's history into a single volume. So, let me apologize now if I overlooked some favorite area or gave short shrift to some other. This book is just an accounting of one experience. Another expedition would undoubtedly produce an entirely different manuscript. Maybe in the future the publisher will send us back to recollect some of the rest.

JEFF DAVIS COUNTY

Driving, the gerund of the verb *to drive* that my stalwart 1966 Webster's Third New International Dictionary Unabridged defines as "management of an automobile or other vehicle on the road." This was a word my wife and I spoke several times a day during our trip, as in, "We're driving to Marathon tomorrow," or, "How long have we been driving?"

Driving is often considered to be a uniquely American invention. The car and all the individual freedom that it offers is as American as a can of Coke. Many travel stories have, at their core, an automobile that is as integral to the plot as any experience or adventure. Kerouac had his Hudson and Cadillac and Steinbeck his "Rocinante." In both accounts, the vehicles were as necessary to the flow of the narrative as any conversation or observation. If the car stops, so does the story.

The car we chose to take on our trip was my wife's 1996 Maxima. If we had owned a truck, we would have used it in an effort to better blend in with the environment. Nevertheless, we worked with what we had. We tried to ignore the high miles already registered on the odometer and instead focused on the leather seats and overall years of reliability. We were going to put the car's good nature to the test. I'll admit, now that the exercise is completed, that the car performed wonderfully, although I think we gave the thing a permanent limp.

The necessity of driving, the labor, the responsibility, the freedom, the excitement, the speed and the constant, slicing forward movement all augment the nuance that is this most accessible modern advancement.

Americans seem, at times, to have fallen faster and more completely than others for this design of individualism and release. We would all be at a disadvantage without the car, and the distances between here and there might become too spread. Further, in Texas, where the expanse of space is famously unbounded, the need for speed is as necessary as a full tank.

Our first destination was Fort Davis, Texas. On previous trips to the Big Bend area, we typically turned left at Fort Stockton and headed south. For this trip, we needed a central location, a "home base" as it were; my wife, with her usual knack for the perfect, chose Fort Davis for its location, history and size. Also, we had not been as far as this before, and the newness of the town hinted at the promise and excitement of discovery.

My wife and I knew well before we ventured out across the vastness of the state that we would be watching much of the area scroll past the car's windows like a panorama. Having driven this stretch before, we were resigned, mentally at least, for the hours of stillness and emptiness. We knew from experience that the reach of road between Austin and Fort Stockton would provide several hours of black pavement and red eyes. So we spent days preparing ourselves. While my wife packed and loaded our cases and car, I pored over maps and books and created a crude sort of schedule of events, writing town and place names onto a simple, handmade three-week calendar. I contacted as many chambers of commerce as towns we planned to visit. Some returned the call or e-mail, and some I am still waiting to hear from. In the few weeks before the trip, I received a couple of press packages from certain towns that were filled with brochures, pamphlets, flyers and more, all expounding on the particular and the peculiar of the area suggested. I discovered, even before leaving home, that numerous museums, historical sites, flying tours, gliding tours, horse ranches, dude ranches, chili cook-offs, *cabrito* cook-offs, salsa festivals, music festivals, water festivals and more waited for our company.

There comes that moment during a trip's planning and packing when you look up and ask, "Is that it?" This is the instant when the worry and concern set in. This is the time when the idea that you have forgotten something crucial begins to germinate. However, try as I might to locate any obvious omissions, my wife had packed with her usual efficiency. Her preparations and foresight border on the professional and prescient. All I was able to scrounge up, after trailing through the house a few times, were an old razor and a half-empty bottle of scotch. Soon, I discovered that the new razor was already packed neatly within the suitcase and that a ten-year-old bottle of single malt was bagged in the back seat of the car, waiting patiently next to the laptop, swimsuits and towels. We were ready to go.

The length of Highway 290 west out of Austin is regularly spotted with weekend day-trippers. This strip of road is studded with parks, vineyards, peach orchards and national monuments. A trek west from Austin will lead you past Johnson City, birthplace of former president Lyndon B. Johnson. Another few minutes will access Fredericksburg, Texas, which is increasingly popular among the weekend getaway crowd, weighted with its antique stores, German restaurants and Biergartens, as well as the National Museum of the Pacific War (Admiral Nimitz was born and raised in Fredericksburg). Additionally, the route, on either side of the town, is fruited with several wineries and vineyards. Many of these wineries have achieved national recognition, and indeed Texas ranks sixth in the nation in wine production. Visitors throughout this area of the state will be sure to find several points of interest, and the entire experience is augmented by the fact that the landscape, the *terroir*, is absolutely beautiful; rolling, green hills, pastures and orchards create a wonderful aesthetic.

In the past, my wife and I have usually had to make the trip to the Big Bend part of the state in the dark; our day jobs keep us tethered to the city until they finally release us at about six o'clock in the evening. Many times we have sailed down the interstate engulfed in the cloud of nightfall. We have always been impressed that much of the road is not lighted and that, after dark, the road seems only to unroll in front of your line of sight. The several yellow deer warning signs along the highway only increase a timorous attitude, for fear of being blindsided by a leaping stag or doe. A friend of mine refers to this too-frequent occurrence as being "buck-shot." However, the likelihood of this accident is much greater on the smaller highways and back roads. If there is a benefit to this constant anxiety, it would be that at least it might keep you awake and more alert. Thus, given the opportunity to travel the interstate during the morning and early afternoon hours was something of a treat for us. The countryside was open, expansive and somehow seemed more welcoming than on our usual trips.

I-10, in the daytime, has a smooth speed limit of eighty miles per hour. Passing from the union of Highway 290 and I-10 to Fort Stockton, Texas, now takes just four hours—bathroom and Diet Coke breaks included. The drive was ordinary for such trips, but "ordinary" entails more than simply sitting behind the wheel watching the world whirl past. For myself, such trips always bring to mind those thoughts that typically grab at my attention in the middle of the night, waking me from a still sleep to wrest from

Limpia Canyon, Jeff Davis County.

unconsciousness to consciousness those concerns that I normally try to cope with under the sun's illumination. During these intervals, when the drive becomes rote, I find that I am designing plans, setting goals and reviewing past accomplishments and failures, trying to learn from each. Many schemes are conceived under the white Texas sun and atop the black, burning asphalt.

We made it as far as Junction, Texas, about twenty-two miles from the juncture of Highway 290 and I-10—or, more to the point, about two hundred miles from Fort Stockton. Meandering through the Texas Hill Country is a beautiful passage. It is also tight, narrow and full of people. The towns are hived with residents and tourists alike so that the streets and sidewalks are teeming with the patter of determination and purpose. Each of those pairs of feet, it seems, also has its own automobile; the effect is that, on any day of the week, the streets and two-lane highways are cluttered with cars and trucks vying for room within a confined area. Because of this congestion, when we entered into the free-flowing range of the interstate, it was as if we had walked onto a sprawling yard after being confined inside a broom closet. Then, feeling freed and relaxed, we needed a Coke and coffee, of course.

Junction, Texas, rests on what seems to be the last hill of the Hill Country and looks down on the highway with a sort of majestic, paternal gaze. It also seems to be facing west, motioning the traveler to do the same. The service station we chose held several antique photographs on the wall in the restroom's hallway. A few showed a parade from 1917 replete with banners, flags, a small waving crowd and several more horses than automobiles.

Another was a pastoral scene of a few persons at a local watering hole. The setting was pleasant but unremarkable. What *were* remarkable were the one-piece, whole-body-enclosing swimsuits worn by the folks in the image. Hard to believe, but everyone in the photo was still smiling, even under the weight of these harsh vestments.

There is a solemnity to the freeway that exists nowhere else. The extraordinary situation of being surrounded by hundreds of others but having little to no real contact with them is akin to walking through Manhattan in the late afternoon. Similarly surrounded, no progress toward anything human is accomplished, save the occasional eye contact. The anonymity of the American highway is both freeing and regretful. A peculiar sort of rejection occurs every time a car is passed and a gaze from the opposite window is averted toward the sterile landscape. We develop sudden, fleeting relationships with those we travel among: remembering a car's make or license plate from one city to the next, children peering through a rear window, the couple silently looking in opposite directions, their conversations exhausted.

I have been fascinated by the idea of where all of these people are going to or coming from—whether they are eager or reluctant about their destinations, whether someone is excitedly waiting for them or if, once home, they are resigned to be as anonymous as they were on the road. It is the same as the airport or bus terminal, except that on the freeway you, too, are among the mobile. As a child of eleven, I would sit in the New Orleans airport (we lived nearby), between my time in the arcade, and watch the crowds fan back and forth. Many times I wondered about the passengers as they stepped from the planes. (This, of course, was during that era when we could still walk to the gates to either wave a friend or relative off or welcome them as they disembarked.) Over time I became accustomed to the expressions of those coming off the planes. I could tell the smile of those who knew that they were expected and the grim, dull non-expressions of those who knew that they were not. It is the same on the highway. Our lives cross, and we come within a few feet of one another; however, the distance between might as well be a mile. Maybe it is the vacuum of the car that is responsible for the isolation. Maybe the shell of the exterior is held, unconsciously, as some sort of emotional barrier. Whatever the reason, we all participate in this scenario, keeping our distance and anonymity secured. However, deeper within the southwest corner of the state, where Texas rests a giant elbow on the Sierra Madre mountains of Mexico, the rules of the road are significantly different.

That portion of the interstate we now sped across was familiar to us even though we had experienced it mainly in the dark. As in so many sections of Texas, the land is the thing. Out past the towns and cities, the land, blessedly undeveloped, reaches out in all directions like some boundless ocean. The notion that all of this country can be owned, fenced and maintained by someone is fascinating. Even with the qualification of cattle, sheep, goats, horses and the lone house pinned on top of a distant hill, it is difficult to imagine that a single person or family can own such a sweep of territory.

Nowhere is this notion more prevalent than in the Big Bend region, where a family might own thousands of acres. If ever there were a need for an example of the breadth of the Texas countryside, this would suffice. However, while we raced through the land, I kept having a thought that was souring the experience, and for a while I could not identify the source of the disease. Then it occurred to me. The impression that the land seemed without border—that its limit could only ever be realized at the horizon, if even there—was disparaged by the reality that it did, of course, have a border and lots of them.

From our vantage point, the territory was majestic, even poetic in scope. A bird's-eye view would bring an abrupt end to such naïveté, for such a position would quickly illustrate the squared, fenced, determined sections of each plot and every plat of property. The poetry would become technical prose at once. While I thought about this issue, I was also struck by the thought that I missed the childish ability to ignore such unattractive truths and to imagine this land as its first inhabitants must have seen it, as the Spanish explorers must have seen it—brambly, semi-verdant, low and sun baked. Undoubtedly those early eyes must have seen the poetry written across the territory and considered it to be just as open and eternal as any child watching the same today from the back seat of an SUV. The vastness of space out here is so empty, so naked, so exposed that one imagines it must be under God's perennial watch.

After passing through the relative oases of Sonora and Ozona (in the evening hours, due not solely to the light cast through the tired darkness, these two towns are most welcome sights), my wife and I glided into Fort Stockton in the late afternoon. I do not remember whether other states do the same, but Texas marks its towns' sizes by the number of exits each might require from the highway. Junction, for instance, is a two-exit town, as in "Junction: next two exits." In this manner, the traveler can determine whether the city or town has the amount of convenience they need to be comfortable. I believe Fort Stockton is a six-exit town; plenty for everyone.

Jeff Davis County

The Davis Mountains.

And like any expanding, modern town trying to stand up straighter and taller than the others in the area, Fort Stockton has dutifully positioned the McDonalds, KFC, its juvenile detention center, Motel 6, La Quinta Inn and medical center along the south frontage road of the interstate for all to witness. The north frontage road holds the service and truck stations. As we passed through, we utilized both sides of the freeway and made notes on the other businesses; we knew that once past here, the level of civilization quickly ebbs to the pastoral.

After filling the tank and grabbing more drinks, we had another forty-five minutes in the good company of the interstate. Once to the west of Fort Stockton, we were in *terra incognita*. My wife, originally from Puerto Rico, certainly had not been this far west before, and my only experience past Lubbock was returning from a memorable Los Angeles expedition twenty-five years earlier. Further, what began to happen just as we passed Fort Stockton was as unusual for us as it was for everyone else in the region—it began to rain buckets. Where the sky before had shown a few clouds, the white sun nevertheless shone on us the entire drive. Now, after leaving Fort Stockton, the sky blackened as if someone had left the fire on under the toast. The clouds, in true west Texas fashion, teeming with water, hung so low to the ground that one felt they might just go ahead and land. In fact, this rain would continue for the next several days. Later we would learn that the culprit was Hurricane Alex, swirling back and forth over Texas. Indeed, after Alex had wrung himself dry over the Texas/New Mexican territories, he was chased out of town by yet another tropical depression that ensured that the rain continued for the better part of two weeks. Locals in Fort Davis and Alpine told us how it was the greatest and most constant rainfall that they had experienced in more than thirty years. We were easily convinced. Even our son, attending college in the far northern Texas town of Sherman, phoned to say that he was receiving the same.

There was a benefit to the deluge. After leaving the interstate for Highway 17 south and passing through the Balmorhea State Park, we entered the Davis Mountains. The road that leads toward Fort Davis here is a winding thread of two-lane blacktop. Behind was the relatively flat steppe of the Pecos area, orogenic detritus from the Rocky Mountain chain. In front and on all sides, the Davis Mountains now rose to tell their story. Stunning is too soft a term to describe these mountains, because they are unlike most others you may have seen. Their aesthetic was enhanced now by the rains. Being July in Texas, where one would expect a dry, arid, dun-colored landscape the region was now virid, even floral.

We were driving the very route taken by the Indians hundreds of years before through this pass. It was this very course on which the Indian guides led Espejo on his trek from New Mexico back to New Spain, now Mexico. This was the course the sheep and cattlemen had taken while looking for greener pastures for their herds. They found them here in the lush valleys. It was this path that the soldiers trod on their way to and from the fort in the nineteenth century. And now, due to the downpours, the entire valley was alive again with green grasses, flowers that had been laying dormant for years and cacti that had all but given up hope. Even "Wild Rose Pass" was sporting several red and yellow flowers like ornamentation on the mountain's lapel. This was our first introduction to the area, and it will forever be the image that we hold.

My wife could not have chosen a better location for our home base than Fort Davis. Pressed against the Davis Mountains, as if induced for a long sleep, the town straddles Highway 118 after 17 appears to dead end (it continues on just to the east of town and continues to flow to Marfa and eventually Mexico under the guise of Highway 67). The purported population of 1,050 is cloaked under the façade of the 100 to 200 who routinely pad the sidewalks and roll the roads. Given that many of those visible are tourists, I wondered if maybe the population's numbers weren't accumulative.

Our motel was on the main street (State Street), and after so many hours on the road, hammered by the heat and roiled by the rain, we were glad for the room, the faucet's cold water and the beds. My outline for the day called

Jeff Davis County

Chisos Mountains Big Bend National Park.

for an expedition into town and fact-finding. However, once the car was unloaded and the room was appropriately apportioned with our supplies, even the Maxima protested further use. We pulled the screen door closed, such as it was, and became quiet for a while.

Sometime in 1581, Fray Augustin Rodriguez, a Franciscan brother, along with a few other missionaries and a small escort of just over half a dozen soldiers, left Mexico and ventured into the territory of New Mexico. By way of a welcome, some of the indigenous Indians killed one of the missionaries. For whatever reason, presumably to fulfill their conversion quest, the surviving members of the church remained; just as inexplicably, the soldiers returned to Mexico, leaving the Franciscans to fend for themselves. Once the soldiers had returned to their base in Mexico and news of what had occurred was disseminated to the community, an effort was mounted to rescue Rodriguez and the others—assuming they might still be alive. Another Franciscan, Bernardino Beltran, was given permission to venture out and try to relieve his brother.

At the same time, a wealthy Spanish cattleman living in the area, Don Antonio de Espejo, asked to accompany the priest. Espejo was to bring along a contingency of soldiers and supplies, as his intentions were not solely altruistic. Espejo's plan was to accompany the priest to New Mexico and to explore the region for his own gain. And so, on November 10, 1582, the expedition set out.

As history has so frequently pointed out, the Fates make fools or heroes of us all. So it was for Espejo when, after reaching the border of New Mexico at the Rio Grande, he and his party learned that the missionaries they were coming to rescue had not survived their decision of the previous year. The Indians had killed them all. At once, Espejo was liberated from this mission and free to explore the territory at will. After journeying as far west as Arizona, Espejo turned east again, and after losing most of his party to some disagreement (most likely the others wanted to return home, since that is exactly what Beltran and his followers did), he continued on toward the Pecos River area. At the juncture of the Pecos with Toyah Creek, local Indians guided Espejo and his remaining men south toward the Davis Mountains. As Jacobson and Nored explained, "Their route passed San Solomon Springs (Toyahvale) and continued to Big Aguja Canyon where it followed an old trail over the mountains to Wild Rose Pass and then up Limpia Canyon. Here they camped at the future site of Fort Davis on the 13th of August 1583."[1] Afterward, Espejo and his men crossed the Davis Mountains and continued on to Mexico.

The journeying of Espejo did little to mark the area for future travelers save announce the region, and the paths through it, for future explorers. Most likely, the greatest advantage to the trip was familiarizing the European face to the indigenous peoples, although even that could be disputed with some vigor. Additionally, the fact that he and his men chose to camp in precisely the spot where, three centuries later, Fort Davis was to be constructed speaks to the condition of the place as ideal for such a founding.

My wife and I found the area agreeable as well. When we woke from our first night's sleep in the area, we found the climate much different than at our home in Austin. When Pat Draheim, a docent at the Fort Davis Historical Society, learned that we intended to make Fort Davis our base while researching this book, she forewarned my wife and me to "be sure and bring a jacket. It gets pretty chilly here, even in the summertime." So, when we woke on our first morning in the town, I was not that surprised to find that I was shivering. A look over at my wife showed that she, too, had been enjoying the local weather during the night; she was wrapped up in her blanket like a butterfly soon to emerge from its cocoon. Encouraged by the thought that our little motel offered free coffee from the store next door, I swung my own blanket off as if opening the curtain to a new scene. (Here, I would like to have made the analogy of swinging the blanket off like opening the door to the morning's cool breeze. However, since our motel room had no front door, only a screen and a "privacy curtain," that analogy just doesn't have hinges, as it were.) I'll not mention the adventure of the metal-stalled communal shower that was home to one of the largest spiders I've seen since playing in the alleys of Lubbock as a child. Instead, I'll just relate that we were soon braced to the morning and acclimated to the climate. The free coffee, which I spiced with chocolate, helped this effort.

We drove down Highway 118 to Historic Fort Davis, which we could have reached by foot in a few minutes had we felt more intrepid. The parking lot, at 9:00 a.m., was near empty, and several park rangers received us when we entered the Visitor's Center. I asked to speak to the park's historian, as we had arranged to meet her that morning. After being told that she was out of town visiting her new grandchild, my wife and I looked at each other, trying to decide our next move. While we debated our alternatives, one of the rangers approached, stood much too close and waited to interrupt. He asked our names and what it was we had wanted with the historian. After explaining ourselves, again, he related that he was "just tryin' to make sure you guys ain't crazy or somethin'!" For a moment, that cold bed seemed warmer than it had an hour before.

Soon, another ranger approached and asked if she could help. After we told her our story, again, she apologized for the inconvenience and showed us all of the literature that the Visitor's Center had. She indicated those areas of the fort that are, literally, in ruins and are inaccessible to the public and those that are restored. She allowed me to leave a note for the park's historian, and soon my wife and I were outside, ready to wander through the remnants of Historic Fort Davis.

Central and south Texas are spotted with towns that were, initially, forts constructed by the United States military. Mainly these outposts were created to facilitate both commercial traffic and settlements throughout the territories of Texas and New Mexico. The constant threat and harassment

Fort Davis National Historic Site.

of the Apache, Kiowa and Comanche Indians demanded action from the United States government if any trade route, mail passage, new village or hamlet held any claim to permanency. So it was that in 1852, Major William Emory, of the United States–Mexico Boundary Commission, made recommendation for the creation of a military installation at "Painted Comanche Camp." Another plea for the same came in 1853 from then inspector general Colonel Joseph K.F. Mansfield.

Based on these suggestions, Secretary of War Jefferson Davis ordered the establishment of a military garrison in the area.[2] The initial site, located nearer the Rio Grande, was relocated to Painted Camp in what is now the Davis Mountains, the official order being directed by Brevet Major General Persifor Smith of the Department of Texas. Nestled up against the jagged, jutting rock, the spot offered the perfect pitch for the fort. It also, to the detriment of a few soldiers, afforded the Mescalero Apaches a perfect vantage point from which to spy down on the fort. Any modern visitor can easily see the advantages from either side. As Barry Scobee, the writer most associated with the area, related, "Indians could be seen peering furtively down from the chimney rocks above the post—and an arrow and the sound of the bowstring would arrive at about the same time."[3] (Barry Scobee Mountain is located on the west side of Highway 17 just before reaching Fort Davis.)

Little remains of the original fort. As visitors will notice, it is quite literally in ruins, and of the original fort, only foundation stones that mark the outlines of old barracks, the camp hospital and officers' quarters are still *in situ*. However, due to the fact that the fort was occupied twice—once from 1854 to 1861 and again from 1867 to 1891—there are several areas on site to visit today. The American Civil War is the reason for the dual occupations. Initially established by the Eighth Infantry of the federal government's forces, these soldiers abandoned the fort in 1861 when the Civil War erupted and Texas seceded from the Union. Confederate forces then occupied the post for a little more than a year until the summer of 1862. From then until 1867, the fort was unused and open to any and all who might try to make it their home.

Those remnants of the second occupation are quite extensive and restored, and they offer a wonderful insight into not only the fort's antique appearance but also daily life during the periods when it was occupied. The row of officers' quarters is itself reason for a visit. The morning we visited, a docent—who turned out to be a schoolteacher from Richardson, Texas, and was dressed in period attire—described the setting of one of the homes for us, detailed daily

Foundation stones of the original Fort Davis.

life, for the wives in particular, and pointed out those items she deemed of interest. In short, she was very helpful and knowledgeable.

One of the stranger aspects of the morning was the visit to the auditorium. Located just behind the Visitor's Center, this small hall proffers a video detailing the fort's history, as well as showing character actors, again in full uniform, describing a day's work in and around the area. Nothing too unusual about that—nothing, that is, until we noticed that the presenter of the video, dressed entirely in a cowboy-red western shirt, a broad-brimmed hat, chaps and boots, was none other than Kareem Abdul-Jabbar, the star guard for the Los Angeles Lakers and Milwaukee Bucks. We knew that Abdul-Jabbar had had several acting jobs both during and after his basketball career, but to find him fronting a presentation about a nineteenth-century west Texas military base was, for myself, extraordinary.

Of course, the reason for Abdul-Jabbar's presence is that the video's producers wanted a prominent African American presenter due to the fact that the "Buffalo Soldiers" held the second establishment at the fort after the War Between the States.

By most accounts, these soldiers had the roughest time out in west Texas. The Indians were more prepared than ever to fight for their land; the citizens of the area, subjected to the federal government's Reconstruction efforts, were not too thrilled with their presence; and the soldiers had onerous daily tasks to conquer. Nevertheless, it can rightly be stated that this second occupation was, by far, the more successful of the two. The camp's remnants

Officers' quarters, Fort Davis.

Early Fort Davis. *Courtesy of the Hunter Collection, Archives of the Big Bend.*

speak to their achievements, as do the twenty-four years that they maintained a presence there. Indeed, their work was so well carried out that by 1891 the government ordered the troops to abandon the fort. The Apache Indians, so long a problem for the ranchers and settlers alike, had finally been driven either onto reservations in New Mexico or south into Mexico. Additionally, the conditions at the fort were deteriorating. The water supply was fouled, and the climate had caused rot under the barracks that was keeping many of the troops ill. Further, the railroad had not made its way to Fort Davis and, in fact, never did. So, with the Indian problem no longer present, the soldiers in constant complaint of sickness and a town unsupplied by any modern convenience, the fort was ordered abandoned in the spring of 1891.

One of the peculiar items about Fort Davis is that it was founded from necessity and abandoned through cause—twice. The years between 1862 and 1867 saw the fort fall into disrepair as bandits, Indians and just about anyone else took what they wanted or needed. After the fort's final surrendering in 1891, the barracks were leased out as rental properties until the 1950s. We learned from residents that these renters had access to the property as a whole (i.e., any one rental unit provided opportunity for the entire fort's land). It is enthralling to imagine what these inhabitants may have discovered during their time on the grounds.

In 1960, the National Park Service made recommendation that Fort Davis be added to the National Registry. By 1961, the Texas legislature had secured the land, and Fort Davis became a National Historic Site. As Robert Utley described in his handbook *A History of Fort Davis*, "Fort Davis is today one of the most complete surviving examples of the typical western military fort to be found."[4]

Once back at the motel, my wife and I took some time off our feet and sat in the wooden deck chairs supplied on the walkway. Within a few minutes, the motel's manager waved hello and said, "Have you guys been to the museum yet? A Ms. Draheim has been calling asking when you were going to get there." Immediately I remembered what I had forgotten. I had told Mrs. Draheim, of the Overland Trail Museum, the week before the trip that I would call her that morning by ten o'clock. It was now noon. My mood began to wane. We had been in town less than twenty-four hours, and already the two appointments that I had arranged had fallen apart like an abandoned military fort.

I asked the manager where the museum was. He turned and walked across the rocked driveway to the side street of the motel. "Yep. Still there," he stated. "End of the block." He pointed up the road and we went to look.

Present-day Fort Davis at dusk.

Sure enough, there it was just two blocks away. If Mrs. Draheim had thrown a rock our way, she might have knocked some sense into me.

As we approached the museum, a woman was trying to unlock the museum's front door. I imagined that the lock might have been as much of an antique as the door and offered to help. "Oh, it just takes some work," she said and cracked the lock with that last syllable. The woman, of course, was the same Pat Draheim who had offered us her advice on the area's climate a week prior. Mrs. Draheim was, without question, one of the most pleasant and hospitable persons we encountered during our time in west Texas. A relatively new resident of Fort Davis, Mrs. Draheim explained how she and her husband had been in town only five years. After visiting Fort Davis a few years before their respective retirements, she told us how, after their visit, they decided that this was the place in which they wanted to retire. She tried to downplay her role at the museum, insisting that she was "just a volunteer," but few volunteers have the subject knowledge or excitement of discovery that she displayed.

Once inside the museum, we were astounded by the quantity of material the place stores. Of the museum's four main rooms, the first houses records of Jeff Davis County—those oversized leather binders that include every bit of business from tax assessments to the sheriff's jail expenditures. I was thrilled that Mrs. Draheim gave us free access to them all, and had I not felt that I was taking too long in poring through the material, I would have stayed there all afternoon. While I read through these journals, my wife inspected the century-old issues of *Ladies Home Journal*, admiring not only the eclectic array of items for sale but also the muted beauty of the full-page advertisements.

The adjoining room was equally entertaining. Within were glass cases of antique toys that Mrs. Draheim told us always fascinate the children who browse the museum. In fact, she related how one young boy recently complained about the frailty of his own toy fire truck after observing a hundred-year-old metal version inside one of the cases.

Also in this second room was a case of old pharmaceuticals—opaque glass bottles of camphor, antiseptics, aromatics and a motley assortment of other remedies and aids. However, probably the most interesting item in the room, certainly the most eye-catching, was a large, forty-star American flag. Dating to the nineteenth century, the placard states that it is the only forty-starred flag in existence. The odd (or even) number of stars on the flag is presumably due to the tumultuous years around the Civil War, when the number of states belonging to the Union fluctuated with prevailing, or possibly local, sentiments—sort of like trying to produce a map of eastern Europe in the early 1990s.

We wandered toward the back of the museum and realized what Mrs. Draheim had already informed us of—the museum was at one time a home.

Overland Trail Museum.

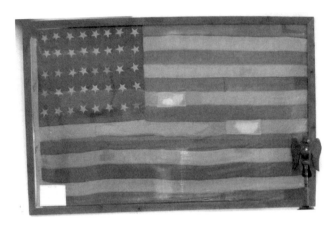

Forty-star flag,
Overland Trail
Museum.

Indeed, the third and fourth rooms of the museum are the bedroom and kitchen of the original house, which belonged to Nick Mersfelder, one of Fort Davis's most renowned, maybe infamous, citizens. Mersfelder was a German immigrant, arriving in Texas about 1881 according, again, to Barry Scobee, who further puts Mersfelder's immigration into Fort Davis only a few years later when he took up residence and opened a barbershop in the same building.[5] The museum is that building, and in fact, the façade displays two distinct entrances: Mersfelder's home on the left, barbershop to the right. The anteroom of the museum still houses an old barber's chair, in remarkable shape for its age. However, Mrs. Draheim insisted that no one knows for sure whether this was Mersfelder's chair or simply another added to the museum's collection over the years.

Certainly *remarkable* is the fact that in Scobee's book on Mersfelder, one of the old photographs of Mersfelder, taken most likely circa 1925, shows him seated in a chair in this bedroom, smoking a pipe and reading. When visiting the museum, one will notice that the room looks almost exactly how it looked then. Indeed, as Mrs. Draheim showed us around that portion of the home, she commented on how a large chest that rests to the side of the room is full of quilts. She knows this because it was she who stored them away. Looking at this old picture, you can clearly see that not only is the chest still exactly where it was, but stacked on top are the very quilts that she spoke of as well.

The kitchen of the house/museum is also extraordinary since, like so much of the home, the utensils are originals—the room appears as though no one save the maid has made a pass though it since Mersfelder's passing in 1939. Mrs. Draheim pointed out a waffle maker on the old stove and said, "This still works. See the handle? It pivots; it turns over."

"No it doesn't," I said, half protesting, half laughing.

"Oh, yes it does," she explained and demonstrated the apparatus by flipping the heavy cast-iron base over inside of its skillet.

"What a thing," I replied. My wife smiled and shook her head.

"I know! It's amazing, isn't it?" Mrs. Draheim replied. She then asked if I wanted to see the basement. I asked if she was kidding. "No, no. Absolutely not. Let's go have a look." After she asked my wife to mind the front door for her, Mrs. Draheim and I walked out back and, after having a look at the old horse stable, proceeded around the house to a locked door on the far side. Again after pushing at a stubborn lock, the door cracked open, revealing a dark passage of concrete stairs. Mrs. Draheim searched for and found the light switch on the wall. Even from the top of the stairs, I could make out a large, dusty room that appeared filled with the flotsam of generations.

Having descended into this cavern, it was soon evident that there was another entire museum under the house. Barry Scobee recounts in his book on Mersfelder that one afternoon Mersfelder led Scobee, a couple of female reporters and another man down into this same basement. There is no time reference in this story of Scobee's; however, it must have been near the same era as the photograph. Scobee relates, "In the cellar we beheld an accumulation of odds and ends, broken furniture, an old gramaphone [*sic*], lumber and a work bench with tools and a quantity of picture framing material."[6] As we moved through the years of gathered debris, I realized that all of those things described by Scobee were still there. The primary difference, the only noticeable change from the past ninety years, was the addition of another gramophone, a few saddles racked on wooden workhorses and a few dozen boxes of books that Mrs. Draheim told me have been left to the museum by the town's residents over the years. "I still need to go through all of those," she lamented, motioning toward the boxes.

As I stood wondering at a decades-old, five-foot-tall curling iron that more resembled a medieval torture device, Mrs. Draheim opened yet another door, this one at the far end of the room. Within we saw stacks and stacks of old wooden folding chairs completely covered in dust and webs. To the side was much lumber, some of it handmade signs but primarily "picture framing material." The floor was bare—the earth *was* the floor— and the walls were simply the base and supports of the home above. I expected bats and snakes but was told that they were not a presence down there. That good news allowed me the confidence to remain for a moment longer to try and imagine those who had placed all of these artifacts in their hold.

Nick Mersfelder's
kitchen, Overland
Trail Museum.

Back inside the house, I wanted to look through the old ledgers some more. Knowing that I would not have access to these books again for many months, maybe even years, it was hard to leave such a treasure. After leafing through several pages of Jeff Davis County's sheriffs' receipts, I found that someone named Lauro had committed a murder and attempted another in the fall of 1933. His trial date was December 26, 1933. Jeff Davis County charged this man $1.50 for the three witnesses needed for his trial that day; however, the other expenses were what really captured my attention.

I felt a little like Holmes trying to piece together a narrative from only receipts in a decades-old ledger. I deduced that this man, Lauro, after committing his crimes near Valentine, Texas, had fled to the El Paso area, where he was later arrested. Jeff Davis County charged the prisoner $0.15 for each of the 226 miles that the sheriff's deputy had to drive to pick Lauro up and then another $0.30 per mile on the return trip. Evidently, having to put up with a felon's company for 226 miles warranted a doubling of the fee. The total for the roundtrip roundup should have been $101.70 (i.e., $33.90 for the first trip and $67.80 for the return). However, the receipt book reads a total of $99.00: $33.00 for the initial drive to El Paso and a flat $66.00 for the ride back with the prisoner in tow. I wondered what could be the reason for the discrepancy.

The schoolteacher in me said that poor arithmetic due to some urge for simplicity was the culprit. However, I considered that even an amount as minor as $2.70 would need to be accounted for in the county records. And besides, three witnesses had been listed at $0.50 each—a paltry sum but clearly one for which some recording was needed. Then it occurred to me; they rounded down. Even in 1930s west Texas, and even when dealing with a known killer, showing some decorum and consideration still had its place within society. Still, in the face of such a horrific event, I had to smile at the reasoning, at the collective consciousnesses of those involved. There was something simultaneously simple yet adoring in this action, a thinking that at once proclaimed duty and regulation but compassion and understanding, too. Here within the yellow leaves of the antiquated ledger was the perfect example of that legendary Texas politeness with which so many of us are familiar and which is, ultimately, borne from an innate respect for the human condition—a $2.70 example set down for the rest of us. I imagined that whoever was responsible for the entry in the book—whether a secretary, clerk or even the sheriff himself—would roll their eyes at the attention I'm giving the item. However, that would speak to the point, too.

Our first full day completed, my wife and I headed to the one grocer in town (very near the union of the highways) and settled into our room with those staples of the displaced city dweller in a semi-rustic environment: sliced ham, sliced cheese, a loaf of bread, a bag of carrots, a bag of potato chips, some Diet Cokes and beer. We ogled our photographs, flipped through the various pamphlets and, most wonderful of all, the several books that Mrs. Draheim had been kind enough to hand to us. Without a television, we made do with our laptop and watched an old Jack Benny video. My wife had never seen Jack Benny before, and witnessing her react to his dry humor and silent, self-effacing expressions was priceless.

Soon the entire town was asleep, and we quickly joined in but not before listening to the stillness after nightfall. I probably shouldn't be so continually surprised by the countryside's lack of urban clamor, but every time we encounter the perfect quietude that so many rural settings offer, it leaves a definite impression. Clearly, the effect is so striking because of the distinctly polarized, and oftentimes sudden, changes to our personal environments. So many have written about the juxtaposition that it seems almost pointless to write further on the subject. For the moment, then, I will try to not be redundant. Maybe it will be sufficient to write that the level of calm and repose afforded by the area around Fort Davis is of the sort that a visitor would hope it to be.

Northeast Brewster County

The Southern Pacific Railroad has as much to do with the settlement of southwest Texas as carbon has to do with the creation of mankind— which is to say, everything. Without one, there would not be the other. Alpine, Texas, drew the steam engine toward itself due to a huge hole in the ground (the Burgess Water Hole) that just happened to be full of the magnet called fresh water. The development of Marathon, Texas, has a similar trajectory to that of Alpine. The ranchers of the Marathon area needed the railroad to stop so that they could more easily get their cattle to market. To accomplish this, they had to give the trains reason to stop, so they, like their neighbor Marfa (which initially held the inglorious but utilitarian name of Tank Town), built a water tower for the steam engines' use. In fact, the railroad's engineers and surveyors were some of the town's first permanent settlers, electing to stay and buy land after their work in the area was completed.

After the rails had been established, the ranchers now had the launching site, as it were, from which to ship their cattle. No longer necessary were the long, arduous cattle drives that frequently witnessed the loss of animals and men alike. Shipping cattle by rail meant more time allowed on the ranch tending next year's herd, or at the very least it meant much less time on the trail away from home. A prolonged, advertised absence frequently was an invitation for rustlers and bandits alike. Likewise, the number of head within the herd could be more properly maintained since fewer would be lost on the trail. As Clifford Casey wrote, "Marathon from the very beginning became an important supply and shipping center for

Cattle chute in Marathon, Texas.

some of the first and largest ranches established within the Brewster-Buchel County area."[7]

The late nineteenth century was the period when so much of this portion of the state was founded, and Marathon is an exacting example of this construction. After the Civil War, many of the settlements in Texas began to prosper, expand and were augmented by immigrants, returning soldiers and travelers from the northeastern portion of the country weary of the constant tumult.

Marathon was, in the 1870s, a "station stop" for the steam engines. The story is that a certain Captain Albion Shepard, a member of the railroad's survey party, mentioned out loud that the landscape reminded him of the terrain of Marathon, Greece. In a way, I can see his point. The immediate area is somewhat flat and dry while just inside the horizon there are mountains and hills, and all are covered with strange green foliage. The only component missing from the Texas version is the sea that is very near the eastern side of the Grecian town and into which the Athenian army drove the Persians after defeating them in 490 BC.

Marathon soon became the shipping center for the entire region. Ranchers of cattle and sheep from all around used Marathon as their deportation spot. And when the quicksilver industry witnessed its boon in the early twentieth century, it was from Marathon that the metal canisters were shipped up north for use, oftentimes, in fuses for bombs and bullets.

We left Fort Davis early in the morning knowing that the trek from Fort Davis to Marathon is nearly an hour and that we would need to pass through Alpine along the way. However, as we had already driven this route once and knew it to be one of the most beautiful paths in the whole of the state, we were looking forward to the drive. The south road out of Fort Davis is Highway 118, and it is one of those smooth, dark gray, meandering cascades of support that every driver enjoys. This section of highway is so lithe, so glasslike, that every conversation within the car is clearer, every radio's song brighter and the wheels seem to whistle as they spin across the surface of the road. This is the sort of pavement that is a motorcyclist's dream—unblemished by ruts, cracks, furrows or crevices. There is not so much as a pothole for the majority of the trip toward Alpine. Further, the drive's enjoyment is augmented due to its positioning within Musquiz Canyon, a valley named for Manuel Mùsquiz, a *vacquero* who chose to graze his herds inside this canyon in 1855.[8] Once outside of Fort Davis and south a few miles, the road begins its wind through the canyon's walls and valleys.

The several trips we had to make on this particular strip of road were notable because of the rains the area was experiencing. Once again, all of the vegetation was more colorful than it had been in years, according to the residents. Every plant that held the potential energy to bloom had yielded to action and was showing with all the character it had to display. The fragrance of the grasses and flowers, the perfume of the wild weeds and those enormous boulders that hang precipitously from the summit of the canyon's walls filled the car, reminding us of their exotic character and reminding us that we were away from home. The few trips we made through this canyon during early morning hours without the weight or impatience of other cars were nothing short of beautiful. There was a feeling of having won some contest, and the drive was the prize, the victory lap. When the conditions are right, and out here they frequently are, a drive through Musquiz Canyon is thrilling.

We drove into Marathon about nine o'clock in the morning, just early enough for the custodian at the Gage Hotel to have placed the yellow "Caution: Wet Floor" sign out on the front stoop. Having a job meant to seize attention, the sign was clearly trying to become the focal point of my camera's shot. We moved on down the sidewalk. I was supposed to meet a local resident later in the morning at the bookstore, and we thought that we could look through some books while we waited. Still later in the afternoon, we were to drive to the famous Stillwell Ranch, Store and Museum. However, that was also several hours away, so we had time to kill.

Billboard for the Gage Hotel, approaching Marathon from Alpine.

It is not difficult to find the bookstore in Marathon. There is only the one, and it is on the main walkway with the Gage and many other businesses of the town.

We entered the store. I told the woman behind the counter who I was and who we were supposed to meet. As it turned out, it was she, the woman running the store, with whom I had spoken earlier by phone. She had told us of this other woman, a long-standing resident of Marathon with whom we should speak to learn about the town's history and maybe even some of its mythology. However, as it turned out, the veteran resident was out of town, and we had to settle for her phone number and an invitation to try and call her later in the day.

I thanked the store's matron, put the number in my wallet and walked farther into the store to have a look at the books in the Texas section—to have a look at the competition. My wife smiled and walked off to see what texts were available in Spanish. I took a book from the shelf, written by a man named Jameson and concerning Big Bend National Park. I sat at a chair in the readers' area and skimmed through the pages. I could not help but wonder if, at that moment, Ms. M. from the bookstore and the historian from the Fort Davis Historical Site might be having a cup of coffee together somewhere. Somewhere nearby. I tried to concentrate on the book instead. I found it useful, well written and concise and made a mental note to try to find it at the Austin library when we returned home.

Remembering that I had not eaten yet, I found my wife and told her, "*Tengo hambre.*" I'm hungry.

We left the bookstore, remembering that a diner had been flashing an "Open" sign when we had driven into town. It was still early in the morning, and we had time to waste and time to eat and relax before the long drive to the Stillwell Ranch. However, it seemed that we were wasting our time too quickly—at least that was the impression given us by a single cowboy camped on the sidewalk.

Seated on a wooden bench in front of a deserted store was a Hispanic man, one I took for a ranch hand. He wore a blue western shirt, dungarees and knee-high leather boots (some call these "snake boots"). Head to boot tip he was covered in the local reddish brown dirt. Obviously he had had a day's work already. He held both arms stretched open like wings across the top of the pew. Making a wide V of his legs, his boots were so far apart from each other that they might have forgotten they were a pair. He smiled as we walked past.

"Most folks don't speed through town like that," he said.

His comment stunned me to a stop. Was he referring to my driving? Was there another car that I had missed? There was no one else, and as far as my own driving went, if he had seen us pull into town, which was unlikely given his vantage point, he would only have seen us parking. Hardly *speeding*. Maybe because I had not yet had my coffee and biscuits with gravy—the biscuits and gravy I was about to get at the diner down the sidewalk with the pulsating *open* sign, the biscuits and gravy that would come with a heaping side of chopped potatoes though the menu had not indicated that any were included, those potatoes that my wife said the waitress, out of the goodness of her heart, spooned onto my plate after looking me over and determining I was in need—I did not understand, at first, what the cowboy meant. After a moment, though, I caught up.

"You mean, we're walking too fast?" I asked.

"Yeah," he said, keeping the smile fixed on us. He added, "Slow down. There's nowhere to be right now."

I smiled. Ignoring his prescience, I agreed, "You're right." We had nowhere to be at that moment except in front of a plate of biscuits and gravy with a healthy side of potatoes.

After our breakfast, which is to say, after my biscuits and gravy and potatoes and three cups of coffee to my wife's one Diet Coke, we walked back down the sidewalk to the Gage Hotel. If ever there was an iconic image for this portion of the state, it is the Gage.

The Gage Hotel, Marathon.

Built in 1927 by the famous El Paso firm of Trost and Trost, Alfred Gage commissioned the building as both a hotel and a headquarters, of sorts, for his 500,000-acre ranch. Like Moses seeing the Promised Land but never stepping foot onto it, Alfred Gage died the year after the hotel's completion, in 1928. Nevertheless, the hotel has remained a staple of the area's attractions for almost a century.

The day we visited, my wife and I spoke with the Gage's general manager. She told us of the hotel's relatively new renovations (a major structural renovation occurred in 1980, with several more adjoining rooms being incorporated off to the west of the original structure) for the hotel's dining room and sixteen "Historic" rooms (i.e., the original rooms from 1927). She laughed in telling us that "there used to be seventeen. But, I took one for my office." She also pointed out that the gym is located across the street (Highway 90), as well as the area where the hotel's chef has his vegetable and herb garden.

As we spoke, the hotel manager's passion for the property became evident. She told us how the "artwork in the hotel is of museum quality." She also described, with warranted pride, how the original portion of the building is made from adobe brick produced "on site." She described the property with obvious zeal: "The attention to detail around the grounds is beautiful. It's just fascinating." She added that the staff is composed, for the most part, of local residents, some of whom are second-generation employees. She called one employee in to speak to us about the hotel's haunted history. Judy told us a story that left both my wife and myself chilled.

Evidently, a few years ago, a couple of children had been left upstairs in their room to rest while their parents were downstairs taking care of the bill. After the children had walked downstairs to rejoin their parents, they spoke of a kindly older woman whom they had met in the hallway outside their room. This woman, the children said, had patted each of them on the head and spoke with them for a short time about nothing in particular, just routine small talk. The children warmed to the woman and wanted to know her name and whether they might see her again. The employee related how, at that time in the afternoon, when rooms are vacant between checkout and check-in, there had been no other guests on the property. Hearing the children's tale, she and another employee went upstairs and found absolutely no one in any of the rooms. The children were unhappy, and the adults became, understandably, uneasy.

Judy also told us that "room 10 is haunted…if you believe." Looking into her eyes that day, I felt that she did believe. In fact, room 10 has a history. In their book *The History and Mystery of the Lone Star State*, Ken and Sharon Hudnall wrote that "guests in room ten have reported hearing ghostly music and sometimes are awakened by a ghost tapping them on the shoulder."[9]

As she was leaving, Judy left us with one last observation. When speaking of a few other employees, she related that "some of the boys won't go in the basement. They say Alfred Gage is down there." She smiled broadly and excused herself.

Just before we excused ourselves that day, the hotel manager spoke of some new renovations that the hotel's managerial partner, a firm in Austin, has planned for the hotel. One of the ideas is to install new flat-screen televisions in each of the original rooms. The hotel manager appeared disturbed by the notion, and I felt the same reproach. As she told us that day, "People come here to experience the landscape, the countryside. They come here to get away from their usual routine and to get some sense of what life was like back then." Flat-screen televisions do not incorporate themselves into nineteenth-century culture with any facility. I could not have agreed with her more. Perhaps the spirit of Mr. Gage will have some influence on the matter.

She waited for us as long as she could, but we were thirteen years too late. The matriarch of the Big Bend, Hallie Stillwell, passed away in 1997 just two months short of her 100th birthday. Today, the Stillwell Ranch, Store and Museum, that oasis of the Big Bend region, is stationed just twenty-three miles north of the Mexican border on Highway 2627 and a hot forty-five miles south of Marathon. As with most destinations in this section of the state, the drive is an effort. However, this was a drive that we made eagerly, if not with some apprehension. It is also a drive we are eager to repeat.

Any drive through this part of the state is nothing short of ethereal—the eternity of the space and the seeming interminable reach of road brought to a more defined reality by the tor scraping the sky at the horizon in the gray-blue distance. We passed an hour or more in this desert dream, woken finally by the sighting of a Stillwell's road sign bleached dull by years of white sun and desert winds.

Highway 385 south from Marathon leads straight into the Big Bend National Park. Just at the northern tip of the park is the cutoff for Highway 2627. This mostly paved road veers to the east and will eventually dead-end into the Rio Grande. A short twenty-three miles prior to crashing into La Linda Bridge, the Stillwell Store rises from the desert dust like a mirage. For myself, at least, driving through the desert always causes some anxiety. I cannot help but imagine car trouble in those areas where I'm least likely to find help.

About thirty years ago, while I was attending college at Texas Tech University, a friend and I decided to be a part of the U.S. Festival, a three-day concert out in the mountains of the Redlands near Los Angeles. We drove. We went through northern New Mexico, which I am told is beautiful, but I wouldn't know since we passed through it during a dark night. We rolled through northern Arizona, where we bought beer at seven o'clock one morning while on an Indian reservation. Later that same day, exhausted by the drive and the desert's brutal heat, we found a spot to pull over and dove into the Colorado River. We both shot out of the river like propelled rockets, being naïve about the water's bitingly frigid temperature.

Later still, and still not finished making foolish decisions, we decided to cross the Mojave Desert in the afternoon. We were told not to. An old man in Laughlin, Nevada, gave us the evil eye and the paternal "don't be stupid" look, but we knew better. We were twenty-one and bulletproof. It was 110 degrees when we left Needles, California.

Several miles into the desert, the car began to sputter. Because we were the only fools out on the highway that time of day, we stopped the car in the middle of the road to have a look under the hood. Being as mechanically savvy as we were logistically, we could find nothing wrong with the car. On the other hand, we did find a twenty-dollar bill impaled on a cactus, a thorn projecting right through Andrew Jackson's forehead. Although, in the predicament we were in, a twenty-dollar bill was about as helpful as a football bat.

We pulled the map out and noticed a black dot of a town just a few miles off the main highway named Essex. We found it quick.

Essex, California, then consisted of a two-pump gas station, a small general store and a mobile home off to the side where the town's one family lived. While the owner of station and town alike inspected the whimpering car, his three small children ran around in circles trying to get the attention of the strangers. Clearly, a couple of new faces were as welcome as a cold drink.

The car's distributor cap was determined to be the trouble, and after some cleaning and adjusting the car was roadworthy again. We drank a beer with the owner, and when I mentioned how much I enjoyed the look of the place, he asked, "Wanna buy it?" Because he was flatly serious, my friend and I laughed about that one for months.

While driving that lonely stretch of highway from Marathon to Stillwell's that morning, the memory of Essex, California, kept coming to mind. Even though I knew the answer, I found that I was continually looking for that black dot town on the map my wife held in her lap. It was not there. We were most definitely alone out there, if you do not count the roadrunners, lizards, cattle, vultures and falcons. Well, one must also not discount the Border Patrol. These dull-green couriers of Homeland Security are as omnipresent as sunburn in July.

The façade of Stillwell Store.

The parking lot of Stillwell Store had a single black truck. Evidently, it belonged to the area's sheriff, since he opened the door for us as we entered. Behind the counter sat a tall, broad-shouldered Texan. Elderly maybe, but the desert sun browbeats all who choose to live out here. This man's bright, smiling eyes missed not a thing, and he sized up the strangers quickly. After the requisite hellos, he called to the back for his daughter; soon Nan Patton, granddaughter of Hallie and Roy Stillwell, emerged from the office area behind the storefront. Nan, like her father—Walter Potter, seated front—has clear, radiant eyes coupled with a personality as warm as the prairie sun. "Oh my gosh!" she laughed. "Living customers!" All at once the room possessed a quilt's comfort. Introductions followed. When I asked if the museum was open, both my wife and I were a little surprised when Nan reached under the counter and brought out a single key hanging from a large wooden handle. She simply handed over the key and routinely explained where the television and DVD player were in the adjoining building—the Hallie Stillwell Museum.

There are, in the Hallie Stillwell Museum, two videos of her life story. Both offer Mrs. Stillwell's reflections on life in the Big Bend area. The Hallie Stillwell saga is as much a part of life in the territory as any mountain range, ranch or other watering hole. Out here, everyone knows how she left her Waco home in 1918 to begin a teaching career in Presidio, Texas, which was, at the time, much harassed by Pancho Villa and his bandits. Her life in the desert took a permanent hold when Roy Stillwell, a rancher twenty years her senior, asked her to marry him. Roy's ranch, a successful homestead effort of twenty-two thousand acres, would be Hallie's new home, her new home for the rest of her life.

One of the many striking points about Mrs. Stillwell's remembrances is her constant comment on her love for the land. She recounts in the videos how she would explore the ranch's expanse, discovering prehistoric Indian pictograms, kicking up arrowheads almost as easily as kicking up dust and unearthing any number of other tools from long-forgotten times. As she stated, "The early history [of the territory] fascinated me." She traversed the land constantly in her early years on the ranch, becoming familiar with

Billboard for Stillwell.

the flora and fauna alike. She and the land had to become acquainted, had to develop a relationship. Her marriage was as much to the countryside as it was to Roy. She admitted that "I had to learn a new way of life. I had to learn *this* country." As for the rest of us, she proclaimed, "If you love this country, it'll love you. If you hate it, you, well, you just better go on."[10]

The Stillwell Museum is a separate building adjacent to the store and RV lodging. Inside the premises, one finds a home complete with kitchen, living room and family area. The latter is where the couch, chairs and television are set up for viewing the DVDs. The space that evidently used to be the living room is now replete with artifacts of the family—photos, furniture and other relics of the Stillwell family's life in the desert. Included among these items are several awards, placards and notices of achievement and recognition. One wall's niche has several photographs of Mrs. Stillwell as Terlingua's "Chili Cook-Off Queen" for several years on. Another declares Mrs. Stillwell the "Queen of the Big Bend." There are many pictures of the family, as any home would have, and more show Mrs. Stillwell with luminaries such as Ann Richards.

A moment's consideration reveals that the entire area could be considered the Stillwells' "museum." The ranch, or what is left of it, begins directly across the highway from the store and extends for 7,400 acres. The other 14,600 acres were sold piecemeal by the Stillwell children (all deceased now) over the years. But still, out here, 7,400 acres is a legitimate, albeit small, example of a west Texas ranch. And what better family could one choose to house a museum, to be a representative of settlement in the area, than the Stillwells? The family has been in the Big Bend region for more than 125 years.

After we had watched both videos, we took one more look around the museum, turned the lights out and locked the door. Catching sight of a healthy-looking lizard, my wife commented on how she could never live in the desert, the number of reptiles being simply too many for her comfort.

Back inside Stillwell's, the sheriff had left for his duties, and only Nan and her father remained tending the store. After Nan laughed that we "must've watched *both* videos," we began to ask about the family and the ranch. Mr. Potter, who told us that he had returned to the ranch in 1983 after many years in San Antonio, described how there are "still a few head of cattle" grazing the land. I asked him who does the actual ranching work, the physical "punching" and herding of the animals. Judging by the look on Mr. Potter's face, the question seemed to have so obvious an answer that

The interior of the Hallie Stillwell Museum.

maybe it should not have been asked. He looked me square in the eye and answered dryly, "I do."

As we spoke, more customers came in—a couple of older women accompanied by a mess of four little girls who were scurrying about the store in the manner of impatient children. One of the women reached into her bag and retrieved a few dollars to hand to one of the girls who had begun to beg for a soda. Mr. Potter, up to then silent, inspected the situation and announced, "That's what I like to see. Women with money in their hands!" I was forever endeared.

After the women had bought their Cokes and taken the key to watch the videos in the museum, the four of us were left again to continue our conversations. Maybe considering that the Hallie Stillwell story was told, Nan started to relate her father's story.

Walter Potter was a seventeen-year-old enlistee in the United States Marine Corps in 1944. Mr. Potter told us how he had tried to enlist at the age of sixteen but that his mother had scotched that plan. After a couple months of basic training, he was shipped in 1945 to the Pacific Theater, where the majority of the military's work still remained.

His tale diverted back to his basic training days for a moment. Mr. Potter began to recall how one of his assignments had been to drive a jeep through sand and mud—a preliminary training exercise designed to simulate the conditions of the beaches in the Pacific. During this training, the jeeps continually failed. Trying to push through the thick, tractionless muck, the clutches burned and became useless, stalling the jeeps.

Now his story leapt forward a few months, and here he was, a seventeen-year-old Texan (known, of course, as "Tex" to his comrades) in a landing craft heading for the beach at the Japanese island of Iwo Jima. When Mr. Potter told my wife and I that his was the first jeep to hit the beach during the marines' first landing on the island, I was fascinated. When he then told us how his jeep had been the precursor to all other machinery and had even been first on the beach ahead of the infantry, I was overwhelmed.

Oftentimes I have read about young men whose first experiences in combat were the D-Day landings. I have often read about such things, and I have always been amazed and even fearful in my own imaginings that this could be someone's reality. That those fortunate enough to survive such a horrific experience would then be consigned to a life with those memories always present has frequently haunted me. I have imagined it often, and now here was such a man standing not three feet in front of me telling us how when he and his partner got the jeep out of the landing craft and started up the beach, of course the clutch burned out and the jeep stopped right out in the open. "We were sitting ducks for the Japanese rifle and mortar fire," he stated. As I tried to imagine what that experience and the following years would have meant to a teenager, my mind was as unresponsive as a jeep with a fried clutch. All I could bring to mind then, as at this moment, was that I was proud to have spent even just a few minutes in the company of such a man.

We all spoke for several more minutes. Nan told us how her mother, Dadie—Mr. Potter's wife and the daughter of Hallie Stillwell—as well as Hallie's other two sons, Roy and Guy, had all passed away between the years 1998 and 2001—holding close together even in their passing. Remembering that Hallie Stillwell had passed in 1997 made these other demises that much more severe for those surviving family members. However, the Stillwells have endured more hardship than most of us will ever know, and they have come through it all stronger than most of us could ever hope to be.

There is much more to the Stillwell story. Some of the tales begin back in the nineteenth century with John Stillwell, a Texas Ranger and father of Roy. A Mexican bandit killed him. There are stories of covered wagons, gunfights

46

Walter Potter and his daughter, Nan Patton.

and, of course, all of the recollections of a family that has witnessed the evolution of the Big Bend area from a vantage point to which no one else had access.

As we were leaving, Mr. Potter and Nan asked if we had been down to the river to have a look at La Linda Bridge. We told them that we had not. Secretly, all I wanted to find was a television, not a bridge. One of the World Cup's semifinal games was to start in an hour. However, after Nan told my wife about the bridge (the two of them had hit it off, and now whatever Nan said, my wife was very attentive), that's where we were headed next.

Mr. Potter had said that the Rio Grande and La Linda Bridge, nowadays sometimes referred to as the "Hallie Stillwell Memorial Bridge," were twenty-three miles south of the Stillwell Store. I'm not sure why I thought otherwise, but the river and the bridge are, in fact, exactly twenty-three miles from the store. I had read that in the nineteenth century the Stillwell ranch had originally been located in Mexico and that, after trouble with bandits and rustlers, the family had moved their operation north to escape not only the aforementioned trouble but also to afford the children a chance at a better education. As we stood that afternoon on the now barricaded La Linda Bridge, gazing out at the Rio Grande and the abandoned buildings on the Mexico side, I was reminded of how—not too long ago, relatively—Texas was a part of Mexico. Indeed, this section of the state was not considered to be a part of the United States until just before the Civil War, and even then that region where we had been exploring was still not regarded as "Texas." It is a sentiment that prevails to this day. To many a Texan's mind, Texas has an emotional border just about at San Angelo. All of the land beyond to the west and south still holds a distinctly Mexican nuance. La Linda Bridge is a fine example of the clashing together of the disparate viewpoints and border realities.

The bridge was constructed in 1964 by Dow Chemical to aid in the transport of fluorspar from Mexico to the States. It is a one-lane bridge, and at least according to the Stillwells, when it was open it greatly facilitated the familial relations between residents on both sides of the border. The bridge was closed in 1997 (not after 9/11, as many consider) due to complaints about smuggling and the violence that so often accompanies such operations. There is an account of a Mexican border guard being killed during a robbery attempt. However, at the time, the bridge was guarded only from the Mexican side, and it was widely known that in order to cross bribes had to be paid. In one of the videos shown at the Stillwell Museum, Hallie Stillwell mentions how the store received much business from truck drivers who camped near the store waiting for word that the bridge was accessible.

La Linda Bridge as it appears today.

There is legislation in the Texas Senate for the reopening of the bridge. And, of course, there are opponents and proponents alike, each with valid arguments. Time alone will determine the bridge's fate. In the meantime, a visit is a must for the adventuresome, if for no other reason than to have a look at the barricaded bridge and the Catholic church that Dow constructed for its employees on the Mexican side of the river. One can just see it out on a lone hill, sun-white with twin bell towers, one for each representative of the riparian congregation. It stands as alone as the bridge that used to grant access. More interesting than its appearance, perhaps, is the fact that no Mass has ever been celebrated within its bleached walls.

3.

PECOS COUNTY

We had visited the Ste. Genevieve winery before. A few years ago, I wrote a number of articles on Texas wineries after becoming interested in the local viticulture industry. Because the Ste. Genevieve winery is, by far, the largest producer of wine in the state, it seemed the natural place to begin a series of papers on the subject. The enormity of the operations at Ste. Genevieve presented the perfect touchstone by which to qualify the other wineries in the state.

A bottle of Ste. Genevieve wine lists Fort Stockton as its place of production. I suppose, technically, that is correct. The winery does have a Fort Stockton address, and there is no other town within several miles in any direction. However, if you're driving around Fort Stockton trying to find the place, you'll be driving for an eternity; it just isn't there.

The Ste. Genevieve winery is, as I've written elsewhere, invisible. Placed along Interstate 10 just off the eastbound frontage road, the building and its ancillary equipment are so nondescript that one would think that the business is trying to remain incognito. And if you do not know what you are looking for, you will drive right past it without realizing that it was ever there. The white, three-story, metal-sided building is huge by standards, but planted within the desert's landscape the structure gets lost among the plateaus, mesas and grasslands of west Texas. The absence of any sign, flag, placard or billboard only serves to obscure the edifice further.

During that first visit, the winery's general manager, Jean-Michel Duforat—a French native of Bordeaux and the 2008 recipient of

The Ste. Genevieve winery.

the Munson Award, given by the Texas Wine and Grape Growers Association—gave my wife and I the grand tour of the facilities. Without exaggerating, I can state that Mr. Duforat was one of the kindest people we had ever had the pleasure to meet. At that time, he had given us so much of his time and had disseminated so much information to us that I was unsure how willing he would be now, three years later, to do it all again. Luckily, he was just as receptive to the idea now as then.

Mr. Duforat was waiting for us as we drove into the winery. I had e-mailed a couple of weeks before, asking to meet him at 10:30 a.m. And so it was 10:30 a.m., and he was standing in the lot waving to us as we pulled in. We walked to his office on the second floor, and he began to fill us in on the recent happenings at the winery. Luckily, perhaps, not too much had changed since our first visit. The winery is still producing more bottles of wine than anyone else in the state. The numbers are so staggering that to compare Ste. Genevieve with any other Texas winery is folly. There simply is no comparison.

Ste. Genevieve rests on a little more than 800 acres of land that are leased from the University of Texas at Austin. One of the peculiar facts about the structure is that, due to the lease agreement, the building is only bolted together and, as such, is capable of being disassembled and moved if ever the need were to arise. Of the 800 acres, the winery is utilizing only about 520 this season. The remaining 280 are waiting for clearing of old vines and retexturing of the soil. Mr. Duforat mentioned that he is hoping to get

The fruit of the vine at Ste. Genevieve.

all 800 acres fully functioning soon. Nevertheless, even with a quarter of the lot unused, the winery is still producing roughly 3,000 to 3,500 tons of fruit a year, which yields about 170 gallons per ton. Altogether this gives about 600,000 gallons of wine per season, and this is a conservative estimate. If this were the extent of the winery's output, that number would eclipse all others in the state by an unbelievable margin. However, the winery also imports grapes, juice and wine from all over the world, countries such as France, Spain, Argentina and Chile. The winery then ages, blends and bottles this juice according to its own specifications—"our own special formula," Duforat laughed—and then ships it across the country. By augmenting its production in this way, the winery is able to export, approximately, an additional 970,000 gallons a year.

All of this wine is stored within the most massive storage facility I have ever seen. Many wineries have one or a few of the standard twelve-thousand-gallon aluminum storage tanks. Ste. Genevieve has more of these than I could count. Additionally, the winery has twenty-eight twenty-seven-thousand-gallon tanks that serve to both age and cool the wine. The size of the unit is almost unbelievable. Walking the rows between these behemoths is an exercise in spatial dimensions. Both times I have visited, I have had the impression of being in some secret, underground military complex; the rooms are dark and cooled, and the metal from the tanks glistens as if alive and breathing, which, if you consider what is occurring inside, they just may be.

The dry storage facilities at Ste. Genevieve are as extraordinary as the production levels and as expansive as the land that it occupies. Stacked floor to ceiling are pallets of cases of wine. One storage room only yields to another as you turn a corner. The movement of the wine, the pallets, the boxes and the bottles is constant. The honking of the forklifts as they approach corners echoes throughout the day. The loading platform is rarely empty. More usually, a semi truck is waiting for its cargo hold to be filled. On the morning of our visit, not only was an eighteen-wheeler being loaded, but two more also waited along the frontage road for their turn at the dock.

Above: Jean-Michel Duforat, general manager at Ste. Genevieve winery.

Left: Titanic wine vats at Ste. Genevieve.

Chardonnay vines with iconic mesa in background.

After several minutes of touring these areas, Mr. Duforat loaded us into his pickup truck, and we all headed out to the vineyard. I noticed as we approached the vines that a new eight-foot-tall fence had been erected since our last visit. Mr. Duforat explained that the deer had become such a constant harassment to the grapes that the company decided to take some action. In all there are six and one quarter miles of fencing around the vineyard. Still, even after the fence was completed, there were so many deer left within the site that hunters had to be brought in to get rid of the animals. Mr. Duforat recounted how there were so many deer after the hunt that they took the majority to Fort Stockton to be distributed among the restaurants, for free.

Driving the rows of grapes with Mr. Duforat is such a gratifying experience because he so obviously loves what he is doing. He knows every row, every vine, by heart. When the fruit is healthy and colorful, as it was this season, he is as contented as a child in a candy shop. When he held the leaves of one vine up so that we could see the fruit ripening perfectly underneath, he was glowing with pride and the satisfaction of a job well done. He knew that the harvest, which was to commence a few short weeks after our visit, would be successful and bountiful.

Several years ago Ste. Genevieve stopped offering tours to the public. The operation is simply too large, the forward movement too constant, to afford the time that tours would take. Indeed, on both of our visits I have felt something of an intruder. However, the time that we have spent at the winery has been as extraordinary as its wines. Luckily for all of us, it has just signed another thirty-year lease with the University of Texas.

After leaving the winery, my wife and I traveled the thirty or so miles back to Fort Stockton. One of the peculiarities of driving long stretches of unfamiliar road is how quickly our minds begin to calculate the progress. The first few trips between Ste. Genevieve and Fort Stockton felt drawn out and distant. Each drive seemed as if the destination was remote and in no way affiliated with the town from which we had left. The connection to things convenient and comfortable, that urban umbilicus, felt severed at about ten miles out. Now, with a few of these trips registered under our wheels, as we drove back to Fort Stockton from the winery the trip had the feeling of association and affinity. Before we realized where we were, we had entered the city's limits—our inner odometers rolling toward routine. We had returned by late lunchtime and arrived at our second goal for the day: the Annie Riggs Museum. The third, if we could make it, was the pool at the motel. We had discovered during our stay that the pool's waters were placid and clear in the early to mid-afternoon hours, those hours between checkout and check-in.

The Annie Riggs Museum is located in the historic section of old Fort Stockton just southeast of the interstate. On our first couple of trips through Fort Stockton, we overlooked this historic area of town because it is set back from the town proper. And since Fort Stockton is the largest town in this section of the state (the population is near eight thousand), it was easy for us to see only what was presented from the freeway. In order to visit the historic parts of the town, you will need to drive into town and even then leave off the main streets. Maybe it is even the fact that once off the highway after a long stretch, one is simply more drawn to the conveniences that a small city has to offer—more coffee than culture at that point.

"Paisano Pete," the second-largest roadrunner in the country, marks this section of the town. Even I, usually not too observant of peripheral things while driving, could not overlook this eleven-foot-tall chaparral frozen in mid-step, the herald of the gate to the town's famous past. Besides, there are typically several folks trying to get a picture with this local icon, and they, too, in their congregating, point the way toward the historical section. The world's largest roadrunner, by the way, is in New Mexico just west of Las Cruces and close to a rest stop along I-10. It is a twenty-foot-tall, motley amalgamation of scrap metal, garbage and old sneakers. The sculpture in Fort Stockton is much more realistic and genuine—although, at eleven feet

Paisano Pete, the world's second-largest roadrunner.

tall and twice as long it is more like a chaparral on steroids, the difference between the two being the difference between Picasso and Rembrandt.

Texas history is well known for its desperate outlaws, psychopathic gunslingers and even a few sheriffs who possessed dispositions as dark as any of their adversaries. While gathering material for this book, I read much about cattle rustlers and horse thieves. I came upon frequent references to notorious figures such as Jim Miller and John Wesley Hardin and had even seen an old photograph of Sam Bass. It seemed that no matter what the subject, stories of shootings, cripplings, gunfights and killings were omnipresent. My pencil was sharpened to scrawl more about scalping, gunfights, posses and Winchester rifles. As a child, I was much interested in these stories, convinced, as children so often are, of the validity of every tale. As an adult, I grew suspicious of the value of some of these stories because at times they seemed as outlandish as any fiction.

So it was as we drove back to Fort Davis that hot afternoon, chasing a lone thundercloud down the interstate. We had just left the Annie Riggs Museum and had seen what the place has to offer. We read that the hotel's name was originally the Koehler, named for a prominent Fort Stockton businessman. We learned that construction was initiated in 1899, the business opened in 1901 and Annie Riggs acquired the business in

1904. We had witnessed the nineteenth-century architecture complete with "gingerbread" latticework, the encircling veranda, the courtyard onto which every door of the old hotel's rooms opened and all the other rooms that were literally teeming with artifacts from the Pecos and Fort Stockton areas. One of the more interesting aspects of the museum is the archaeology section that features a Columbian-period mammoth tusk. Other areas include rooms devoted to ranching, religion, business, geology and pioneers. By standards, the museum is a large building, and every room is filled with remnants from the surrounding territories. It is a true treasure-trove of memorabilia, and the photographs that accent every wall of every room will make any visit worthwhile.

While driving, as so typically happens at such times, I began writing, mentally. After a few minutes, I was hoping to be able to enliven the subject somehow. I knew that I would need more research to tell the museum's story completely and adequately. What I did not know, or expect, was that the Wild West was about to rush across my page with all the bluster and violence of a stampede.

There is a portion of the Annie Riggs story that is not mentioned in the brochures, but many people in the area know of it nonetheless. That Annie Riggs's full name was Annie Stella Frazer Johnson Riggs and that her second, and last, husband, Barney Riggs, was a notorious, trigger-happy drinker is common knowledge among those literate in the territory's folklore. However, the Barney Riggs story is inextricably linked to that of Annie Frazer's, and all who hear it will never be able to see the museum in the same solemn light again.

The interior of the Annie Riggs Museum.

To start at the end, Barney Riggs died at the Koehler Hotel on April 7, 1902, presumably with Annie Riggs, who had divorced Barney the year before, at his side.[11] He had been shot in the chest by Daniel "Buck" Chadborn. Mr. Chadborn was the son-in-law of Annie Riggs, having married a daughter from Annie's first marriage to James Johnson.

Barney Riggs was born in Arkansas in 1856. Soon the family moved to Texas, and by the age of eighteen Barney had already killed a man in Salado, Texas, just outside of Austin. The killing was ruled accidental, but the stigma of "killer" became a constant moniker of Riggs's.

At the age of thirty, now living in Arizona, Riggs again was involved in a killing—this time it was no accident. Returning from a "cattle-buying trip," family and friends told Riggs that his wife, Vennie, had been seduced by Riggs's stepcousin, a man named Richard Hudson. When confronted by Riggs, Hudson denied the accusation, and for a while all appeared smoothed over. Evidently, though, Hudson could not remain silent about such a conquest, so Riggs made a conquest of Hudson. The report states that Riggs waited for Hudson until evening and then shot him several times from a concealed location. Indeed, the jury nearly found just cause for the killing, folks in the South having a soft spot for the cuckold, evidently. However, the fact that Riggs had hidden in the dark instead of calling Hudson out, like a true southern cuckold should have done, tipped the scales in favor of life in prison at the infamous Yuma facility.

Just under a year after his incarceration, a prison riot sprung Barney Riggs. During the melee, Superintendent Thomas Gates was taken hostage at knifepoint. What followed were several minutes of absolute pandemonium wherein prisoners and guards alike ran for cover, crawled wounded across the exercise grounds and dove for safety behind anything offering shelter. The whole time, the tower guards showered bullets down on the convicts, leaving several dead. Barney Riggs, after coming into the yard from the tailor's shop where he had been working, saw the superintendent locked in what could have been his final struggle. Gates called out to Riggs for help. Riggs grabbed a pistol from a guard-shot rioter and mortally wounded the man who was holding the warden hostage, saving his life. This prisoner, however, already twice shot, still managed to stab Gates in the back—a wound so severe that a lung was punctured. Sadly, Gates survived this attack only for a short time. The knife attack had been particularly savage, and the wound pained Gates deeply. Because of the injury, Gates was forced to step down from his position at the penitentiary the next year. A few years after that, unable to withstand the constant pain, he took his own life.

For Riggs's one act of bravery, C. Meyer Zulick, the governor of Arizona, granted a full pardon. The pardon came with the stipulation that Riggs "[l]eave the territory forthwith and never return thereto."[12] We can't know for certain, but I suspect that this stipulation was about as necessary as a flat tire. Riggs walked out of the Yuma, Arizona prison a year to the day after he had been locked up.

Riggs left Arizona and ventured to California, where his wife was waiting with their son. After more marital trouble, Riggs soon left California with his son but without his wife. It is interesting to note that no divorce was ever recorded for this marriage, which leads to the supposition that Riggs's next marriage to Annie was bigamous.

Barney Riggs married Annie Stella Frazer Johnson, who was also divorced, in September 1891. In the course of their decade-long relationship, they had four children. But Riggs had finally met his match, as it were, in Annie. As DeArment wrote, "Annie's family, the Frazers, had a long history of violence rivaling that of the Riggs clan."[13]

Annie Riggs endured several years of violence now. Barney Riggs was arrested several times while the family lived in the Fort Stockton area. He became known as a "bully" and someone to avoid. He treated his wife no better than he did the residents of Fort Stockton. Annie Riggs filed for divorce but soon retracted the motion. It was, however, only a reprieve for the marriage.

There are several stories of abuse, most of it drunken in nature. The final straw for Annie seems to have been when Barney poured coal oil on her clothing with the intent of setting her aflame. She filed for divorce a second time. She stuck to this decision, and the couple was divorced in March 1901. Additionally, Barney Riggs was court ordered to pay $2,000 in child support. And here begins the end of not only Annie and Barney Riggs's relationship but also the end of Barney Riggs.

Daniel "Buck" Chadborn was the name I kept seeing when doing a modest amount of research on the Annie Riggs Museum. After some searching, I found that Mr. Chadborn had become a well-respected law enforcement officer as an adult and lived until 1966. Although twenty-one years old, Chadborn was assigned by the court in Fort Stockton to oversee the support payments from Riggs to Annie. Because of hostility and small-scale violence (Riggs beat Chadborn with a cane at one point), Chadborn asked to be taken off the assignment. However, even having put this distance between himself and the situation, Barney Riggs's insults and threats, against Annie and Chadborn alike, continued.

The day of his killing, Riggs was in a saloon and through a window noticed Chadborn packing Annie Riggs's things into a buggy. Enraged, Riggs crossed the street to confront Chadborn and Annie. Sheriff Bob Neighbors, however, noticing the scene and, sensing the potential violence, told Riggs to leave his gun at the bar. Riggs obeyed and strode out to confront Buck Chadborn with his cane. Witnesses reported that Riggs raised the cane as if to strike Chadborn. Reaching for the revolver he happened to have on the buggy's seat, Chadborn shot Riggs.[14]

The only part of the story not already mentioned here is gruesome, and I'm reluctant to relate it. However, now I must.

Without a doubt, Barney Riggs knew a deathblow when he saw one—he had dealt a few himself after all. Riggs must have known right away that he was killed when Chadborn grabbed his revolver from the wagon, turned and shot Riggs in the chest. Riggs struggled with the wound, turned away and staggered awhile. As he dragged off, his life pouring into the dusty street, Riggs tried, with his only available resource, to staunch the flow of blood by plugging the hole in his chest…with his own finger.

The mental image is not pleasant. It could be that one is not as grieved as I in the hearing of this, but the fact of the tale cloaks the hotel in a slightly moribund aura. Who of us now will ever be able to see the museum in the same way again? But this is the truth of the matter, and much of the history out here expresses a similar violence.

Annie Riggs, with the funds made available from Barney Riggs's death, bought the Koehler Hotel in 1904 and changed the name to her own. The property was run as a hotel and boardinghouse until 1931, when Annie Riggs passed away. From that time until the 1940s, the hotel was operated by a son, Ernest, and his wife. From this time until 1955, the hotel housed other family members and continued also to be run as a hotel. In 1955, the family handed the property over to the Fort Stockton Historical Society. It has been a museum since.

This was the history that we walked into that morning. The front door was unlocked and the sign read "Open." We continued in. There was no one behind the counter, so we were free to inspect all of the bric-a-brac that was hanging from the walls and piled along the countertop. Even from the front door, it was easy to imagine this place as a hotel or boardinghouse. The open rooms and the expanse of the space spoke to the period's architectural style.

We passed through the dining room just beyond the entrance and came to the kitchen. This room was cluttered with hundreds of culinary items. Because any of these things could have been originals, I stood wondering if

The Annie Riggs Museum.

that cast-iron skillet had ever been thrown at Annie Riggs by her psychotic husband, if that coffeepot had ever been knocked and spilled during one of their infamous fights or if this was the breakfast table that had heard the early morning's comment that had led to an afternoon's drunken brawl. We had already noticed, from Fort Davis, that the relics of an area typically stayed within it, so I felt confident that probably several of these kitchen utensils had seen some action through the years.

We wandered around a few more minutes but never found a soul. As we walked back toward the entrance, we passed a couple of painters. They were headed toward the back of the museum, where their work waited, and I figured that was where the employer must be, overlooking some new construction. Besides our car, the painters' truck was the only other vehicle in the lot that morning.

The Annie Riggs Museum is located in the heart of Historic Fort Stockton. Directly across the street is the grand Pecos County Courthouse. In fact, the entire "Historic" section of Fort Stockton is located on the same side of town as the museum. The actual fort of Fort Stockton is a couple of blocks away. The town's chamber of commerce has listed seventeen points of interest for those visitors wanting to spend an afternoon, or two, touring the remains of the old town. A blue and white marker identifies each of these historic sites. The whole could be seen in a day, although the summer's white heat might demand additional time.

Founded formally in 1859, Fort Stockton was created, much like Fort Davis, to offer protection both for the early settlers, ranchers and travelers and for the Butterfield-Overland mail service that operated a route through the territory twice a week. Fort Stockton's initial settlers congregated at the spot because of the abundance of water that flowed from Comanche Springs. Indeed, archaeological evidence indicates a settlement near the springs dating from several thousand years ago. A small community near the fort, settled by Irish immigrant Peter Gallagher and termed St. Gall, was eventually incorporated into Fort Stockton after the residents had a change of heart about their masthead.

Again, similar to Fort Davis, Fort Stockton was garrisoned from 1858 until 1861, when the start of the Civil War demanded the abandonment of the fort by Federal troops. And just as with Fort Davis, the CSA troops took over the fort, but only for a short time; they had left by the end of 1862. At the war's conclusion, Federal troops once again took possession of the grounds and set about reconstructing the fort. This second effort is about half a mile from the original location, where the Pecos County Courthouse now stands majestically at the end of the historic section of town. The new occupation lasted for nineteen years, from 1867 to 1886. This second withdrawal lasted until the community of Fort Stockton took control of the land and had the site added to the National Registry of Historic Places in the 1950s.

Fort Stockton is named for Commander Robert F. Stockton, grandson of Richard Stockton—a signer of the Declaration of Independence. Born in New Jersey in 1795, Stockton would make his way south after enlisting in the navy and participating in the War of 1812 at the budding age of sixteen. Stockton had a very successful military career, noted especially for his service during the Mexican-American War when he led campaigns in California. He was so successful, in fact, that not only is there a Fort Stockton, Texas, but there is also a Stockton, California (named by himself for himself—no doubt taking a cue from Alexander the Great and perhaps even Peter Gallagher). A borough of New Jersey also bears this name, as does Stockton Street in San Francisco. Additionally, another "Fort Stockton" rests near San Diego, an actual fort that today is eroded beyond ruins. A rest area on the New Jersey Turnpike also claims the Stockton name.

Pecos County

Of the seventeen historic sites outlined by the city, the old Pecos County Jail is one in remarkably fine condition. Constructed in 1883 from the sandstone native to the area, the structure today is a wonderful site to visit. The top floor, where the iron cell doors still hang open for tourists to enter, is open for inspection. Dark and grim, the cells are still marked for segregation with signs of a 1950s vernacular that I am reluctant to repeat here. The bars separate only portions of space, and each cell is joined to the next. Even those separated by the walkway are still within spitting distance. Walking through the jail that morning, it was easy to imagine the din that would most certainly have been constant. It was easy also to imagine the stench the jail certainly exuded when in operation. The compartments have only small metal toilets and sinks. Although the cells are small, they had the capacity to contain up to four persons at a time. The stale, putrid odor, the noise, the confusion and chaos that would have existed within those walls when the cells were at capacity must have been a magnificent hell for all involved.

The bottom floor is a showcase for sheriffs past and present. One wall displays photographs of sheriffs and deputies from the nineteenth century to the present. Other items in the room include a gun case with vintage firearms, an antique desk that belonged to a Pecos County sheriff and other law enforcement items such as holsters, revolvers, a very small but authoritative sheriff's badge and a pair of period iron handcuffs that are so severe they appear punitive just hanging from a peg on the wall.

The morning we arrived, three very pleasant and helpful volunteers who were cleaning the front door and porch area greeted us. After we entered, the use of each of the downstairs rooms was explained, and we were allowed to tour them at our leisure. Most of these rooms belonged to the sheriffs' families and included a sewing room at the far end of the building. I am reluctant to refer to this as a residence due to the jail upstairs; however, the bottom floor—save the front room, which was obviously the sheriff's office—really could be described as nothing else. The volunteers explained how the sheriffs' wives and children lived and played in the building just as any family would—just never mind the couple dozen prisoners upstairs yelling from the barred windows for someone to throw them a cigarette or deliver a message. My wife asked whether the prisoners' noise often bothered the families who lived in the building. One of the volunteers offered an old anecdote by way of answering.

The time must have been from the early to mid-twentieth century. The sheriff of Fort Stockton and Pecos County (Fort Stockton is the county seat) was out of the house/office/jail for the night on assignment. The sheriff's wife and children were left to mind the house and jail. (Where the deputy or jail's warden were is anyone's guess.) Upstairs, in the jail, were several men who had been brought in on charges of disorderliness aggravated by alcohol. About dinnertime, the prisoners began arguing and swearing at one another. Then they began howling from the windows at whoever was below, outside. With her children already nervous from the uproar, the wife called her husband to ask what he could do to calm the situation. His reply was for her to try and take care of the situation by herself. Evidently, the sheriff included some remark about how if she could handle and raise their three children then certainly she must be able to control a few locked-up drunks. She walked upstairs.

The sheriff's wife was, by this account, young and attractive. Her appearance inside the jail was well received. The prisoners answered her request for quiet and order with more jeering. The wife retreated downstairs, served her children dinner amid the clamor and thought about the situation. The sheriff would be gone all night, and the pandemonium upstairs could not be trusted to run itself out of steam.

As it turned out, the answer to the problem lay just outside. With dinner over and the children put to their places in the bedrooms, the wife walked into the backyard and found the garden hose.

The stairs of the old Pecos County Jail run from inside the building's back door. It is a straight line to the cells above. The cells, likewise, are arranged together in a relatively open space—that is to say that the jail is really a large room that has been cordoned off by rows of bars. The only walls are those for privacy between the bars and the toilets, and these are simply stunted, short sections of board. Standing from one strategic position just inside the main door, one can see all of the cells from front to back. From this location the wife was able to wash away the problem with only a moment's worth of showering. She and the family enjoyed a quiet rest of the night.

The next morning, the sheriff returned to a soaked jail floor and several cowering, shivering prisoners. Of course, he asked what had happened. Her laconic reply was, "You told me to handle it. I handled it."

Whatever the veracity of the tale, it is a fitting story not only for the jail and its stone-hard façade but also the whole western nuance, that stalwart individualism that pervades the region.

I have heard and read of many travelers who have had an experience similar to that of my wife and me, namely that in passing through Fort Stockton they overlooked the historic section of town. It is an easy thing to do. Not visible from the highway, the old town is easily missed by travelers to this "way out west" town frequently because they are more in need and desire of coffee and gasoline than sightseeing. Nevertheless, the effort should be made. Not only is the old jail chilling and slightly exhilarating to examine, but the fort, the Riggs Museum, the Comanche Springs Pool, the Pecos County Courthouse and St. Joseph's Catholic Church have also been marvelously restored and maintained. The pool, in particular, is an enormous public watering hole that resides next to the old Comanche Springs—the main reason for the area's initial settlements. In recognition of the springs' significance for the territory, every July the community hosts a "Water Carnival" wherein the town enjoys a little cooling off in conjunction with picnics, parades, music and other festivities. The carnival was established in 1936 to commemorate the Texas centennial. Soon, however, due to a few ranchers' greed, the water supply was cut off when these few pumped the groundwater up and out for their own use, literally drying up the pool and likewise denying the life-infusing water for other farmers and ranchers. In 1951, the carnival was canceled for lack of water. Maybe not surprisingly, litigation about who has rights to the groundwater is still flowing through the Texas Senate. Still, it is a wonder to consider, while swimming in the chill, relaxing waters, that this same water source has been utilized for thousands of years.

The pavilion was constructed in 1938, as were the bathhouse and pool proper. The water's flow, said to have raged from the earth "like a sea monster,"[15] was stamped out by years of overuse for irrigation. The "monstrous" springs ceased flowing by 1961. The good news is that in recent years, even beginning as far back as the mid-1980s, the springs have delivered small amounts of water once again. The accrual seems sporadic, seasonal even; however, some is a better sign than none. Apparently, nature is trying to overcome the damage done by a few of its offspring.

Intermittent but heavy downpours interrupted our tour around Historic Fort Stockton that day. The residents were glad for the rain. After a few minutes of the showers, it seemed that more people had moved outside. The heat out here can be so brutally oppressive that the local population cheers anything that is able to battle it successfully. While the drop in temperature was pleasant, the gray and dark afternoon did little to help our photographs. We loaded up and headed back west toward Fort Davis.

A few miles southwest of the intersection of Interstate 10 and Highway 17 lay Balmorhea State Park. Similar to Comanche Springs, the reservoir is now a large pool area. We had heard much about the beauty of the place, and we were eager to have a look. We also wanted to have a swim to escape the heat and the exhaustion that it brings. However, the

A downpour near the Big Bend National Park.

rains, this time accompanied by serious lightning flashes, had followed us from Fort Stockton. When we passed by Balmorhea (which you must if heading down to Fort Davis), we noticed that it was still open but that no one was swimming, presumably because of the lightning. Although it was four o'clock in the afternoon, the skies were dark gray, and the clouds, as they do only in west Texas, hung precariously low to the ground—full of life, full of biting energy. We decided to return to Balmorhea later in the week and continued on to the motel, hoping that the pool was unoccupied and shimmering in the sunlight. It was. We spent an hour relaxing by the motel's pool, scanning through the day's photographs and marveling at the landscape; one peak of the Davis Mountains reached up from behind the motel as if surging forward. We watched the traffic, or lack of it, on State Street, Fort Davis's main avenue. Even by Fort Stockton standards, the level of calm and repose here is extraordinary. And so we spent the remainder of our afternoon, my wife with her Caribbean, olive skin soaking up the sun as if a sponge and me, with my northern European pallor, soaking up a sunburn.

4.

Northwest Brewster County

Many years ago, my son and I drove from Austin, Texas, to Rhinebeck, New York. Along the way, we passed through Tennessee, the long way, west to east. I remember that the highways there were as smooth as glass. We had come to these roads after being jostled and jarred by the potted and cracked highways of a couple of states before. Even though we drove a new car, the ride bounced and shook us for several hours. Then we came to Tennessee, and the freeway was all at once calm, like the sea after a violent storm. Later still, I would read Senator Al Gore commenting on how well-maintained Tennessee highways are; it is a source of pride for him and the state.

Adding to the great relief we felt, we noticed that all along the highway were large and inviting rest stops. After passing a few, we decided to stop and have a look. After all, when traveling with a ten-year-old, any time to stop and romp around is a good thing.

The rest areas in Tennessee were, and I hope still are, expansive buildings full of information and utility. The grassy lot surrounding the place was just suitable for my son to run through, and the Civil War–era cemetery that lay just off to the side was the perfect accoutrement for a young boy whose only thoughts on the subject had come from the glory-filled pages of history books or the drama of movies. For this reason, for him the cemetery held the nuance of the imagined brought into view and not the reminder of destruction that they so frequently do for those of us who are older. The real treat, however, was inside the rest area.

Once we had finished staining our shoes in the grass, we headed indoors and were surprised to find that there was an older man seated behind a counter. "Good evenin'!" he nearly shouted. He seemed genuinely pleased to see us. He asked where we were from, how long it had taken us to reach Tennessee and where we were headed. All of this information appeared important to him, and we were comfortable with him because of his interest. Soon, he surprised us further by offering cookies, coffee and Kool-Aid. Never before had I been welcomed and fed while visiting a rest stop. In Texas, the most luxurious of them offer vending machines that are not yet stripped of their items. Maybe the toilets are clean, and the garbage has been carted off. But here was a whole different animal. This area was catering to the traveler and seemed to know and anticipate his needs and desires even before he had felt the drag of a long drive fall away. Soon we felt that we were at his home, and when it was time to leave there was a sense of regret. We found ourselves planning to return as soon as we had left. And when we had left the state and entered into Virginia, there was again, rising from the pavement through the wheels, the near constant bite and muffled roar of uneven asphalt.

Up the interstate about twenty minutes from our home in Austin is a new and engorged rest stop. This industrial-sized rest area has been fed on the milk of tourism and its subsequent reconnaissance. The population of Austin, and its satellites, has increased by several hundreds of thousands in the fifteen years we have lived here. The city has literally overgrown its boundaries, and the result is the destruction of its infrastructure. The water pipes are bursting; the streets are fractured; there are regular, small-scale power outages; and the traffic has gained national infamy. All that was attractive, all that tended to be a draw for the visitor, has been trampled into extinction. It is a horrific irony that those elements that helped make Austin such an attractive town have been eradicated in order to offer housing for those who moved here to be among them. The rest "mall" that has been constructed just north of town is, then, a sort of way station for those in transit to Austin—a last stop to check the bindings before the final unloading. And therein lies the difference between the two—the one here and the stop in Tennessee. The former serves as a terminal marker, the Coke and chip stop before moving in. The latter, for all its comforts, is clearly designed to offer only temporary accommodation for those passing through.

I illustrate these two dichotomies to serve as foils and to stand as contrast to the most perfect rest area I have ever passed through.

When leaving Fort Davis for Alpine, Texas, on SH 118, there is a rest area that begs travelers to stop no matter what the purpose of the trip. Consisting only of a couple of tables, benches and one of those iron grate grills, this stop is settled under a sheltering canopy just off the road's shoulder. The space here is adjacent to a large pasture, and on the morning that we first stopped, the owner was mowing his field due to the heavy rains the region had just experienced. Even though he and I were separated by about a hundred yards of green grass, he still caught me looking from across the way and waved a good morning to me through the grate of his tractor. Several head of cattle roamed just behind.

Fort Davis is one of the "mile high" towns, and that morning, again because of the rains and the altitude, the air was calm, cool and still. We stood outside of the car and breathed in the countryside and its entire atmosphere. It seemed strange to me to have found so much character in that one location and to have identified the region by this one, lone divot in the road. But there was something about the placement of the rest stop that was unusual. It was proffering no concessions and did not seem to be either welcoming Fort Davis visitors or saluting those leaving. By all appearances, the place was created only because that section of road, with its tranquility and verdancy, demanded some inspection from those who would pass by.

This area of the state is not short of scenic views and overlooks. Indeed, just a few miles outside Fort Davis, but in the Marfa direction, SH 166 intersects SH 17. Highway 166 is a forty-three-mile scenic loop running through the Davis Mountains. The road was built, beginning in 1933 and completed in 1939, for the sole purpose of granting access to and bringing about appreciation of Davis Mountain State Park and its surroundings. Any stop along this stretch is a wonderful opportunity to view the local scenery, and it is all well worth the attention. Nevertheless, the rest stop on SH 118 is

The Davis Mountains
after a rain shower.

unique in its isolation. It is entrancing with its silence, and if you are driving toward Alpine, as we were that first morning, it even invites a visit knowing that you have just begun your trip.

Through the course of the next few weeks, as we drove to and from Fort Davis, we passed this rest area several times; rarely was it vacant. No matter what the time of day, the place was almost always occupied, and those resting in the shade always appeared to be in the same lazy trance as I had been that first morning, answering some siren's vision.

Terlingua, Texas, hosts an annual chili cook-off the first weekend of every November. It is a big deal in this part of the country, and thousands of people drive from all over the country to either participate or, like us, watch all of the excitement.

The crowds for the cook-off accumulate slowly during the week. Aficionados arrive early in the week, and others, mostly the spectators, drive in after work during the weekend. However, like a bad relationship, getting in is easy…it's the leaving that is hard.

The chili cook-off officially ends when the band stops playing early Sunday morning. Typically, there is also a large, open-fire cookout that accompanies the music and signals the end of the festivities. All of this means that come early Sunday morning there is an exodus from this little town that would make Moses proud. Unfortunately for those in a hurry, there is but one highway out of town, and from sunrise onward this one vein of road is clogged with every RV, camper, truck, trailer and car that made the journey. SH 118 is the one line out of Terlingua, and it heads directly to Alpine. From there, it is still another hour to the interstate. More than once, having failed to keep our plan of waking early, we have been unhappy members of a makeshift convoy, pouting participants in a motley parade. If the pouting is too severe (usually endorsed by the previous night's beer), we search out breakfast in Alpine and try to waste some time. It was during the first couple of these stopovers that we noticed that Alpine was actually a very pleasant and vibrant community. We had, like our experiences with Fort Stockton, overlooked the town's charm and history in our desire to reach another destination. Lesson learned: slow down, take a look.

During that first week of our trip, what we needed in Alpine were the services of the library at Sul Ross University. More specifically, I needed to browse the archives at the library in order to see what photographs it might have on file to accompany these pages. The authors of almost every book and article I had scanned or read about this part of the state—or even Texas as a whole—made

The Jeff Davis County Courthouse still in July 4 regalia.

mention of the great help they received from the archival librarians at Sul Ross. We had sent some e-mails back and forth, and the librarians had offered direction on how to access the archives themselves (the descriptions of the photographs are available online). By the time we left Austin, I was already eager to meet the women in charge of the collections.

We left Fort Davis early one morning and, after the stop at the rest area, continued on out SH 118 through Musquiz Canyon. The morning's breeze, after yet another thunderstorm the previous evening, was cool on the skin, smelled of earth and dew and grass and seemed to cleanse the car's interior as it rushed through the opened windows. Maybe not surprisingly, the memories that such odors recall are often those of childhood, when a day's personality is recorded forever because of its newness, its freshness and delights.

As we came to Alpine, we passed the town's small airport. Normally, we would have driven right past and not thought too much of it. But that morning brought a somber thought to both my wife and myself.

On the day we had arrived at Fort Davis, July 5, the flags were still flying from their poles, hanging on about every door and awning in town. The banners were still rolling in the wind, and spent firework shells littered the streets. We also noticed that the flags on the larger buildings were at half-staff.

The news, the terrible news, was local. No dignitary had died, nor head of state nor even state politician. We learned that there had been a plane crash in the very early morning the day before. The plane had been one of the medical service flying an elderly woman, her husband and two paramedics to a hospital in Midland. The craft had taken off from the Alpine airport just after midnight. A few eyewitnesses reported seeing the plane attempt to gain altitude but with no success. One observer said that he saw the plane begin to fall through the night's gray air and flame pursuing the tail and then an explosion. The sheriff's deputies reported that the plane had hit a hard, dried rut in a field while trying to land; it flipped over and burst into flames. Speculation suggests that engine trouble led to an aborted takeoff and an unsuccessful emergency field landing. No one knew the cause of the crash (there is still no word), and the knowledge of it spread a pall across the entire vicinity. The pilot and one of the paramedics had only recently moved to the Fort Davis area. The patient, the woman whose broken hip was the reason for the flight, had recently triumphed over a yearlong battle with breast cancer.

A few days later, I was surprised when the manager of the motel where we were staying asked whether we had gone to the memorial service for the crash victims. Initially, I was flattered to think that we were considered enough a part of the community to participate in such a solemn and personal occasion. However, I told him that we had not since we did not know them and had not been invited by anyone. My answer appeared to trouble him. We asked if he had gone to the service, but he stated that he had been too busy. Evidently, a motel, like a mind, must remain open.

Like so much of Texas, Alpine is undergoing growing pains. Construction is everywhere, and the streets, in particular the highways and main thoroughfares, are being widened to accommodate the influx of residents and tourists alike. So as we drove into town, being familiar with only one route to the university, I naturally became lost. If not for the fact that Sul Ross stands on a precipice keeping a wise watch over the community, I would probably still be driving around looking for the library. And it was raining.

Alpine is, like many small college towns, aligned on a grid of one-way streets. Denton, Texas, supports a similar layout. And now that the one one-way street I was accustomed to was closed, the yellow detour arrows that pointed to the correct path were as foreign to me as any ancient language. The sheer number of them was dizzying. So, I did what I always do when I find my eyes darting in opposite directions while my mind treads the proverbial fool's pool—I asked my wife for help. Her reply was quick, laconic and terse: "You just passed it." I jerked my head around, an effort that seemed to have been just what it needed, and sure enough there was, or had been, the entrance that the librarian had e-mailed me about. Within a couple of minutes, we were pulling into a parking spot directly under the windows of the archives section of the Bryan Wildenthal Memorial Library at Sul Ross University.

There has always been something uniquely fascinating about old photographs. Old manuscripts, too, possess the same magic, as do certain works of art. Antique photographs and daguerreotypes are extraordinary relics. They are not memories but rather progenitors of them. The light and the life captured on the silver plates exude an animation that is matched only by actual experience. Emotions are frozen at an instant, an expression forever real and available for inspection, refusal or acceptance.

There is a certain element of voyeurism in examining photographs—in particular the early ones, when the foreknowledge of experience had not yet become a component of the still, and hubris and narcissism were not yet the photograph's constant companion. That is to say, the subject had not yet had the years' worth of viewing other's pictures and was not so totally aware of what the product would become. Nineteenth- and early twentieth-century photographs possess this quality. Often the subjects peer at the camera as if unsure what to expect. Many of these pictures hold truths that are adorable, tender, horrific and heartbreaking. Nowadays the photographer needs to furtively sneak around to try and catch his subject unawares in order to obtain the honesty that these photographs portray so easily.

Manuscripts likewise contain these same elements of personality. Whether text transcribed onto velum, papyrus or crude wood pulp or a handwritten letter, the handwriting thereon is as much an indicator of personality as any picture. The texture and pressure of the line and loop and the draw of scrawl across the page illustrate emotion as well as the words they represent. A paleographer I know has told me more than once how she believes that she is able to determine a scribe's mood and even his health by the way his letters are formed on the page. She has even gone so far as to claim to be able to ascertain where one scribe left off during a sentence or word and another took over. Probably the most famous example of this type of occurrence was when a certain paleographer, working at the Vatican, claimed that he could pinpoint the moment one scribe had died while transcribing a text and another took over at that juncture in the manuscript.

Works of art pose similar adventures. Anyone who has examined a Van Gogh up close has seen the insanity and fervor of genius literally cresting from the canvas. Oftentimes the paint is not so much brushed on as piled and then pushed around with another utensil or finger. Inspection of a Jackson Pollock will yield a like experience.

All of this is to say that in most works of art, a certain level of bravery, honesty and illustration of life's condition is displayed. And, again, the older the photograph, the more likely the depth of expression to be found. Genuine emotion and honesty stare back at us through the decades, and our task then is to try and understand the statements.

The archives at Sul Ross curate thousands of just this sort of inhabitant wealth. Created by the university in 1976, the depository is a treasure of information, ideas and intellect. Families, organizations and individuals have bequeathed their photos and letters and such to the university over the years, and now the archives is the possessor of one of the greatest collections of southwestern artifacts in the world.

Sul Ross University is not a difficult target to hit once within Alpine's city limits. The college rests atop a large hill at the east side of town, and its famous red brick exterior is visible from most vantage points. Named for former Texas governor Lawrence Sullivan Ross, the college was established by state legislation in 1917. Sul Ross State Normal College began conducting classes a few years later in 1920, the delay being the interruption of World War 1. According to the university's documents, "Seventy-seven students enrolled in the summer of 1920. They studied education and liberal arts subjects leading to teaching certificates and junior college diplomas."[16]

Sul Ross State Normal College was the successor to the Alpine Summer Normal School, an institution dedicated to preparing students for teaching certificates. It may be surprising to learn that until the 1970s in Texas, teachers were not required to have college degrees. The only requirements were a certain number of college hours and a satisfactory score on a state exam.

Both the citizens of Alpine and professors of Sul Ross realized that they had a unique institution in an extraordinary location. From the beginning, the curriculum has mandated that students have interaction with the land around them. The university has aligned its vision with the territory; graduates are certain to have studied and had contact with the desert, so that the flora and fauna are as integral to the diploma as any textbook. The opening statement from a Sul Ross bulletin dated from 1939 makes the case: "The courses offered at Sul Ross attempt to make the fullest possible use of the natural advantages of the area." And farther down reemphasizes: "Students are attracted to the study of anthropology and geology here

Sul Ross University.

because this region is one of the world's richest natural laboratories for such studies. Nearness to historic forts, watering places, and old trails make the study of Latin-American and Southwestern History doubly attractive at this institution."[17]

The university has also kept pace with the agricultural advancements within the state. Students of botany and geology have for decades attended classes at Sul Ross to be near the eclectic wonders of the Big Bend region. Nowadays, with the wine industry in Texas blooming, Sul Ross is offering course work in enology and viticulture. A constant connection to the land is a prerequisite, it seems, for involvement with the college.

The morning we arrived at the archives room, I immediately understood why so many other writers have praised the librarians who work there.

The archives section of the university's library is small relatively but, in its relative seclusion, is perfect for its purpose. Inside the large wooden doors we found the reading room, a space about the size of a good living room, with several tables—some elongated for map viewing—complete with all of the accoutrements necessary for the scholar or student: printers, magnifying lenses, scrap paper, boxes of sharpened pencils and more. A long counter separates the reading area from the materials section, and the amount of space afforded for this is an instant indicator of the amount of material the library has in stock. The shelves, which are stacked with boxes and journals and papers, extend far back into a building that appears to be one of those semi-industrial locations that hides the employees within its vault. This morning, however, Jeri Garza, associate archivist at the Archives of the Big Bend, greeted me and my wife. I introduced the two of us, but because I had called a couple of days prior, Ms. Garza had been expecting us and, true to a librarian's sense of order and timeliness, already understood who we were. In fact, not only had she presciently recognized us, but she had also already pulled several boxes of materials from the shelves for us. Some of the things were those that I had found online and e-mailed her about, others were those that she had pulled down in anticipation of our visit. Coupled together, the load on the counter would take hours to peruse.

We spent two days at the archives, thumbing through the photographs. Ms. Garza and the chief librarian, Ms. Bell, pulled box after box for us.

There were forms to fill out in order to be able to handle the pictures. No one was about to hand over these priceless original stills without some sort of identification, some sort of responsible stamp. Ms. Garza was as patient as a saint as she showed me how to complete the forms. Your name here, your address and phone number there. What is your purpose with these? Who are you with? What is their number? Address? Is this a private article? A research paper? A book? Well, who's the publisher? What's your deadline? And so it was for all. And as I fumbled and blundered my way through their forms and certifications, both librarians smilingly helped me correct all of my errors that I am absolutely certain made them cringe on the inside. Each box of photographs had a strict regimen of protocol for its acceptance. Lot numbers, bin numbers, collector's name, family's name and collections all had their own peculiar code and device for access. The librarians knew each combination. But they would confess the codes and grant the containers only after the proper sequence of forms and identifications had been called for. I felt like a schoolboy again asking for my first text from the library after dawdling through the note cards for a while, trying to appear proper and concerned. But of course, I was concerned. I was very eager to have a look at the history of this place. I could feel that these boxes held mysteries that were as foreign to me as any other distant land. But the mysteries, when focused through examination, became real, became obviously near. These people were not aliens; they were my neighbors. They could have been my family.

You can't believe what some of the collections held. So many were pictures of the Big Bend. Grandiose, magnificent photographs of the mountains, valleys and streams, some now extinct, and deep, echoing canyons. Some of the flora were beautiful stills of cacti in water-filled bloom or parched near death, sage, flowers and grasses as strange as any on Mars. Others were of the animals that one rarely sees except when stopping and waiting. One was of a mountain lion, large, tawny and powerful even in death, facedown in the water, drowned having slipped into a smooth rock watering hole and unable to leap or claw out.

But most of the photographs were those images of family and neighbors—the heat-hammered faces of the long-enduring, the river-washed, the sun-hardened; they all stared back through the years, waiting for recognition. The marriages, the quinceañeras, the wakes and funerals, all vested in the finest available. Flowers adorned every such picture. Even the cemeteries warranted close inspection because of their ornamentation. But the faces...so many grasps to the past. Their visages stared ahead as if knowing we would be looking back 150 years later. These people stared into the camera lens as if looking through a portal. They were not waiting for the explosion of the flash but rather the propulsion of their image into the future—our present, our here and now. And there they were: the cowboys in their leather and dirt and those prurient smiles; the women in dresses so stiff and severe as to be less than feminine. There are pictures of gunmen, wearing their holsters forward so we can all see how fierce and ready they were to kill.

We came upon photos of the Ku Klux Klan perched on horses. Even the animals' faces were cloaked, and I'll be damned if I can think of why. Except, perhaps, that the shame of their hatred and their vanity was too much even for themselves.

There were so many pictures of families that it would take another book to tell of them. Clearly an element of great importance in the early settlements, the family unit was as necessary as it was useful to the home and the ranch or farm.

In all my wife and I spent two full days at the archives. We pored through the boxed collections and had them scattered about the tables along with our notes and folders. Another time, the maps were laid out, exposed and spread on the elongated tables. Some of these are truly works of art. The surveyors' and mapmakers' meticulous attention to every detail was fascinating. Every mountain range, valley, gulch, peak, trench, river, stream, inlet, watering hole and draw was indicated with precision. Several of the earlier maps were, of course, hand-drawn, and the thought of how long these works must have taken was amazing. If there were mistakes, they were unrecognizable to us.

When we had finished our business with the archives, we walked through the university's grounds. At the back end, we found the Museum of the Big Bend, a building of natural rock construction that showcases the history of the entire area, from early civilizations to the present. The afternoon we spent there, we were the museum's only visitors, but it was summer break; the only students to be found on campus was a group of wide-eyed freshmen on an initiation tour.

The museum was originally built in 1937 by design from the offices of the West Texas Historical and Scientific Society. With some funding from the Works Progress Administration (WPA), the museum was opened soon afterward.

The museum is a treasure of information regarding the native Indian, Mexican and early settlers' cultures. The day we visited there was an exhibit entitled Faith and Devotion: At Home with the Saints. This collection was set apart from the museum's main collection of artifacts and included several Madonna icons, as well as Mexican *retablos* and *ex-votos*, small religious paintings on tin canvases. These works, many dating from well over a century, were marvelous examples of religious artwork and offered a clear picture of the Catholic influence in the region.

As my wife and I wandered the museum proper, we took note of the permanent collections. In the back is a full-sized chuck wagon and harness hitchings; old neon signs from the Alpine area hang suspended from the wood ceiling; and off to one side was a glass enclosure containing items belonging to Dan Blocker, "Hoss" of the television series *Bonanza*. Yes, the tan, suede cowboy hat that he wore on the show was included. It sits alongside his jersey from his days playing football for the Sul Ross team. A photograph of him from those days shows him towering over two other players as they posed together, arms interlinked at the shoulder.

Museum of the Big Bend.

The Museum of the Big Bend is as important an element to the Sul Ross campus as the campus is to the town of Alpine. The town has become a college community. However, as mentioned before, it was the water supply that initially brought the Indians, the Spanish explorers and early settlers to the area.

The water's source, the "Water Hole" as it is known, has had several different names throughout the ages. The "San Lorenzo," "Charco de Alsate" and the "Burgess Water Hole" were all early terms for the waters. Nowadays the name "Kokernot Springs" is used; whichever the name, it was the water itself that shaped the area.

Once the water supply was made common information, farmers and ranchers began moving through the area grazing their stock. It was not too long afterward that the railroad made its way into the region, and that construction has been the keystone, the permanency marker, for most of the towns in the entire southwest region of the state. Indeed, the Southern Pacific Railroad first raced through the area in 1883, through a town that was named, at the time, Osborne.

The name Osborne was soon changed to Murphyville when Thomas O. Murphy, of the Fort Davis area, bought several sections of land in the Alpine Valley and the town of Osborne. When the Texas legislature designated Murphyville as the county seat, many ranchers and farmers were made unhappy by the designation, as it was many miles from their homes and ranches. Soon the name Murphy lost its cachet. As Clifford Casey wrote in his history of the area, "The Murphys, for whom the town was named, lived in Fort Davis and were not overwhelmingly favorites of the people of Murphyville."[18] As dissatisfaction breeds action, the citizens of Murphyville—either because of a reference to the area resembling the Alps of Switzerland or due to the odd fact that Texas had no town called "Alpine," as did several other states already—circulated a petition for a name change, and in 1888 the area officially had the moniker Murphyville changed to Alpine.

Alpine is, like every town in the region, an oasis of sorts in the desert. Smaller than Fort Stockton but larger than its sister towns of Fort Davis and Marfa, Alpine has quite a history in the area. Its inclusion of the Sul Ross campus is certainly one of the main reasons for its prominence. However, as with so much of this section of the state, it has its share of old western gunfight lore. One story in particular has haunted me since the afternoon I first read of it by the pool at the motel in Fort Davis. Truth be told, the tale stays with me even today.

In the mid- to late nineteenth century, when ranchers first began to bring their herds to the area, and the grasses were still "knee-high to a horse's belly," one of Alpine's early settlers was a Civil War veteran named H.H. (Henry Harrison) Powe. This man and his wife had been some of the town's earliest settlers and, from all evidence, a couple of the area's most upstanding residents. The pair were charter members of the local Methodist church, and Mr. Powe was an original member of the "Men's Bible Class" and Mrs. Powe of the "Women's Society of Work" of the First United Methodist Church.[19]

H.H. Powe had served with the Thirteenth Mississippi Regiment during the war. At the Battle of Bull Run, Powe was wounded just above his left elbow. Doctors could not save the limb, and Powe was forever after a one-armed man.

After the war, Powe, his wife and nephew came to Texas and eventually settled in the Fort Davis Mountains area. Powe began to raise cattle for a living, and the couple nestled into the community, well respected and well accepted. How, then, could this man who was a founding member not only of the First United Methodist Church but also the town of Alpine itself be murdered less than two decades after arriving in the state? Sadly, the answer is "all too easily."

It was January 1891. The ranchers of the Alpine area who possessed the smaller ranches in the area decided that several yearlings had become spread around the territory and that it was time to gather and sort them out. They planned a roundup for January 28.

As usual for things relating to this area in this time period, Barry Scobee is the event's chronicler. From his vantage point, in 1952, Scobee was able to sketch an account of the day Powe was murdered by speaking with several of the people who were either at the roundup or had direct connection to it. His main resource was a letter written by Powe's son, Robert M. Powe, who as a teenager had been with his father the day of the killing.

The younger Powe relates how, during the separating of the few thousand head of cattle, a "brindle bull yearling" was found among the cattle but obviously without its mother. H.H. Powe considered that the brindle bull belonged to himself, and a few of the other ranchers agreed. Under any other circumstance, that would have been the end of the discussion. However, one of the larger ranching groups, Dubois & Wentworth, had sent an agent whose job was to make sure the other ranchers branded none of the Dubois & Wentworth cattle. The man they sent was named Fine Gilliland.

As the elder Powe cut and separated the brindle bull into his own herd, Gilliland decided that, for whatever reason, the yearling belonged to

Dubois & Wentworth. Strangely, Gilliland had even asked a few of the men present, the teenaged Powe among them, to whom the bull belonged. The unanimous answer was Powe. The answers did not satisfy Gilliland, and he began efforts, with a lasso, to drive the bull away from Powe's herd. Seeing this, Powe rode his horse over to a friend, Mannie Clements, and borrowed a revolver from Clements's saddlebag. As Gilliland was still trying to cut the yearling out of the Powe herd, H.H. Powe aimed the gun and shot near the bull so as to scare it back toward his own group.

Gilliland evidently took this action as violence and reached for his own gun. A couple of shots between Powe and Gilliland followed, resulting in Powe's wounding. Both men dismounted at that point, and while the one-armed Powe tried to steady both his aim and horse, they stood facing each other only yards apart. The gun Powe had borrowed from Clements had just three shells in the chambers, and he had already fired two of them. Only the Lord knows if Powe was aware of this sorrowful fact. Both men shot again at each other, and apparently both missed.

At this point, Gilliland ran to where the wounded Powe stood, grabbed the empty revolver from his hand and fired, point-blank, into his chest. The younger Powe writes how "Father staggered a few steps and fell on his face, dead." Gilliland, cognizant that there were several witnesses to the murder, grabbed the nearest horse and rode out quickly. What happened next is as inextricable as the gunfight itself.

Some of the men whose job that day had been to do the actual branding of the cattle, after they were divided among the groups, got a hold of the brindle bull that was the cause of all the violence and branded the word "MURDER" on one side and "January 28, 1891" on the other. From accounts, this bull would forever be ostracized by other cows, often to be seen wandering grazing fields alone until one rancher bought the animal and headed it north, along with the rest of his herd, to Montana some years later.

A few days after the Powe killing, two Texas Rangers, Thalis Cook and Jim Putnam, on assignment to find

Gravestone of H.H. Powe.

Powe's killer, came upon a man riding through the mountains alone. They stopped to ask him his identity, and the response was a shot from a revolver that shattered Cook's knee. The next shot killed his horse. They had found their man.

Jim Putnam drew his Winchester rifle and fired, killing Gilliland's horse and toppling Gilliland onto the cold ground. As Gilliland took cover behind the dead animal, Putnam crouched and waited for a target to show itself. Slowly, Gilliland raised his head from behind his horse's rounded chest. When enough of Gilliland's forehead was exposed, Putnam put a rifle's cartridge through it.[20]

I only came upon this story recently, and I do not know why, after reading all the other tales of drunken gunfights and outrageous violent brawls, this particular tale stays with me. Maybe it is the one-armed thing. Maybe my mind feels compelled to feel pity for Powe because of his obvious disadvantage. Maybe it is because the brindle bull appeared to be, in actuality, Powe's property and because the whole thing is another tragic misunderstanding that took the life of a well-meaning and respected man. It is most likely both.

The more I read the story from Scobee's little book, the more I realized that more information was needed. Unfortunately, not much more was forthcoming. All other accounts were not nearly as complete as Scobee's. On the other hand, while reading through a website one evening (I do not remember which one, a terrible testament to my journalistic abilities), I did read that H.H. Powe's grave was located in the Alpine cemetery. Being so close to the town, I became very excited about the possibility of locating the marker. Had I learned a little more, had I taken the time to learn the names of Powe's descendants, I may have discovered that some still live in the area.

Normally, I am not a cemetery walker. Except for the flower-filled history of the old Ghost Town Cemetery in Terlingua, I will avoid them as I would a wild animal, choosing instead to find my moribund pleasures in the obituaries of the newspaper. But having read about Powe's grave and finding ourselves in the town with regularity, we decided to drive out and find the marker.

The afternoon that we left the archives at the Sul Ross Library, we asked one of the librarians where the Alpine cemetery was located. The directions she gave were very nearly correct—though the street she indicated was a one-way and had a dead end before the cemetery was reached. Nevertheless, when we came to the street's end, where a few lonely homes stood that clearly dated to the '50s and '60s and were in some disrepair, we could see that the town's farther area, where the cemetery was likely to be, was just *over there*.

We pulled the car alongside one of the cemetery's gates; seeing a man standing among the graves and watering the grass, we thought we would ask whether he might know where to find Powe's grave site. It was a long shot, but so many of the town's residents seemed to be familiar with their own history; there was a chance, in my mind at least, that he could point us in the right direction.

As in so many instances when the obvious appears to be waving to me from a near position, if I go to greet it and shake its translucent hand, it is gone like a phantom. It happened here as well. When we approached the man who was tending to a few graves, we waved, said, "Good afternoon" and expected the same. Maybe his thoughts were on those beneath his feet; maybe he was standing among friends or family and his mind was just not with us. Whatever the reason, when we made ourselves known and asked our question, we received an open-mouthed, blank stare followed by one of the slowest shrugs of the shoulders I have ever witnessed. It was as if his shoulders had slowly filled with helium on cerebral command and risen accordingly. We left him to his work.

That would have been the end of the encounter; we would have walked away, never to disturb this man's somber thoughts again had we not then been attacked by the cemetery's demon. This Gorgon came snarling and howling through the thick grass with a vengeance that was at once terrifying and hair-raising. We would have run to the hills, but a closer look exposed the Harpy to be nothing more than the man's diminutive terrier. The little dog came close but always balked just out of boot reach, yapping and clamoring his prattle. I called to the man to take control of his animal, as it was snipping too close to my wife's shoe. He turned his head and called the dog's name in such a soft voice that the message to the terror was not to *heel* but rather *why not continue to do what you want while I stand here tending the dirt*. He returned to his watering of the hard, hot ground. The dog continued to hound our steps, but as I coiled up a good left foot, it left off its chase. Obviously familiar with the pointed end of a boot, he retreated back to his human. I was left wondering why the man's dog was so much more garrulous than he.

My wife and I meandered through the cemetery for several minutes in the brutally hot July afternoon. Finding nothing useful and no one else to ask help from, we returned to the car and drove into the far portion of the cemetery, and it was there that we noticed that the cemetery is divided, divorced or even segregated. The back half of the Alpine cemetery was cloaked more in flowers, real and plastic alike, and the graves were marked not only by stone but also with candles, bottles of wine and liquor, religious icons and even children's toys. Friends or family had obviously made some of the markers, wooden planks with handwritten slogans or large rocks painted with names and dates and remembrances. Clearly we had found the Catholic plots; the vast majority was Hispanic heritage.

All over the world, United States included, I have seen cemeteries where there is a distinct separation between the Jewish population and all others. This is such a common finding that it leaves no imprint anymore. However, the both of us were slightly surprised to see so obvious a segregation between the Protestant dead and their Catholic neighbors. If funerals are for the living, then certainly this arrangement is designed to deliver some particular message as well. I think its message is one I would rather not hear. Nevertheless, the demarcation, such as it was, indicated that we were in the wrong section of the place if we wanted to find Henry Harrison Powe's grave. We loaded ourselves back into the car and drove within the cemetery's waist-high walls toward the front section where we had initially started our search.

I found some shade and parked the car. Soon, we were wandering the site again. We came across several gravestones that resembled what we thought Powe's would be (i.e., those small, rectangular white marble markers that are as laconic and stern as the men they identify). These seem to have been favorite choices in the late nineteenth century. I have seen them from Pennsylvania to New Mexico.

Straddling concrete boundaries, I walked through the graves, reading the sad indicators of sad news. And then, as so often happens, my wife came to the rescue and called to me from across the grass. She had found the cemetery's plot map, and there, listed with hundreds of others, was H.H. Powe's name—plot 6C. As it happens, we had walked right past it a few times without noticing.

Powe's grave is located within a larger section that contains other family members. He had had a couple of children, and while I knew from my reading that his son had moved to New Mexico, I also had read that his daughter had married and remained in the Alpine area. Wilson was her married name, and a couple of markers here held this name.

Powe's grave now has two markers. One is a small, dark metal plaque, maybe eight by fourteen inches, and the inscription is brief: "H.H. Powe," and the initials "C.S.A.," the abbreviation for Confederate States of America, under the name. Just below this metal plate is another marble stone that is slightly larger and appears more contemporary. The inscription on it reads the same as the original but has more details about the man.

There was no indication at the cemetery or in the inscription as to who might be responsible for the second marker. Whatever the reason for the second placement, I was very pleased that my wife had found the site. I stood longer than was probably necessary staring at the grave and remembering the horrid story of his death. I found that I wanted to know the rest of the tale. I wanted to know what had happened to his widow and children. How had they gotten along after Powe's murder? I had read that the children were young; the boy, at least, had been only a teenager and a witness to the killing.

There were no answers to have, and I had to resign myself to that fact. The only other news I have been able to discover is that the rifle used by Ranger Putnam to kill Fine Gilliland had been in the possession of an Alpine resident in the 1950s. The story I read about that weapon stated that the owner of the Winchester had intentions of handing the weapon over to some local museum. However, I do not know whether this happened or where the rifle is today. Likewise, Barry Scobee wrote that he was in possession of the Confederate coat that Powe wore the day he was shot at the Battle of Bull Run. The coat's left sleeve was torn from cuff to elbow, the result of some doctor's attempt to get at the wound. Scobee also wrote that his intention was to hand the jacket over to the West Texas Historical and Scientific Society of Alpine. In his book on the subject, Scobee wrote, "I presented it to the Institution after Mrs. Wilson [Powe's daughter] gave it to me in 1935 for that purpose, to preserve it as a historical relic."[21] As written earlier, the West Texas Historical and Scientific Society is today the Museum of the Big Bend on the Sul Ross campus. My wife and I visited the museum, but I have no memory of the coat being there.

When we left the cemetery and passed the front entrance again, the same man as before was still standing in the same spot, still watering his dirt and grass. His half-pint hellhound, that demi-Cerberus, came charging out to attack the car. I honked to keep it from falling victim to the wheels, and the monster skittered away. The man did not so much as turn his head.

5.

PRESIDIO COUNTY

Writing in one of the Sul Ross State College bulletins, the writer J. Frank Dobie, when discussing the "regional writer," commented that "[t] here is no higher form of art and, therefore, no higher form of patriotism than translating the features of the *patria* into forms of dignity, beauty, and nobility."[22] I was pleased with his choice of the term *patria* as it indicates so much more than simply the land where one stands. *Patria* is a Latin noun that the Romans used to describe not only their territory but also the very idea of it. The word denotes every nuance, characteristic and element of the land; *patria* nourishes, cherishes, cultivates and educates. It is the reason you go to war and build your tall walls. The word's etymology is in the word *pater*, or father. As such, *patria* is the originator of all that your community is; it is the very essence of the society.

The term *patria* and all that its use translates into would certainly have been agreeable to the native Indians who first inhabited this section of Texas. This race of people was as connected to the land as any can be, and they left their mark, their claim, for all to see. The mountains are full of their pictograms and petroglyphs, the representations of their experiences in the land. Hallie Stillwell, during her many years wandering in the desert on her ranch, used to speak of finding just such etchings and paintings on the rocks of caves and canyon walls. Many other writers have written of similar experiences out here. The local residents, too, have seen them, have sought them out and incorporated the idea and ethos of them into their daily lives. Adherents of Jungian philosophy would undoubtedly argue that contemporary residents carry this ancient spirit within them.

Presidio County

My wife and I knew of these pictograms and had seen the pictures and read the stories. But just as I have always wanted to find an arrowhead but have never known just where, exactly, to look, I did not know this time either where these illustrations might be hiding in the mountains. As luck would have it, the motel's manager was familiar with the local landscapes and had grown up around and within it; when we mentioned that we were interested in seeing some of these pictograms, he was more than happy to oblige.

We had discussed driving out to see these petroglyphs the evening before as we sat around the motel's pool. In the morning, we loaded into the car and drove out Highway 17 south of town heading toward Marfa.

The scenic drive through the Davis Mountains, Highway 166, connects to Highway 17 just outside of Fort Davis on the south side. We turned right on 166, heading west onto this road, and passed about twenty minutes before pulling over into the first rest area we found. The motel's manager led us to the barbed wire fence separating the rest stop from the ranch land and, knowing just where the wire was its loosest and open, pulled the strands apart for us to climb through. I asked how he remembered the spot, and he laughed, "Oh God! We used to come out here all the time when we were kids. I've been all through this country."

He led us up a thin dirt path that wound around the cacti and trees and past the boulders that had, at some point in time, fallen from the mountain we were ascending. After a walk of about fifteen minutes, he led us up into a cave, the mouth of which gave a fantastic view of all the proximate ranch land; the day was clear, and we could see for many, many miles out into the desert. The manager, gazing out onto the terrain, said, "You know, every time I look at this, I think of the people who were here first and think about what they must've experienced looking from this same vantage point." He pointed to a very narrow, dun-colored trail that wound from the base of the mountain we were standing on out across the desert for miles and then disappeared into the hazy horizon. "That trail was made by the Indians thousands of years ago. They walked that trail constantly looking for food and water. And, there *are* water holes out there, and they knew where each one of them was. A lot of those water holes are still there, too. That's the same trail the Spanish took when they got here, and it's the same trail the early settlers of this area used and it's the same trail the ranchers use today."

"That's amazing," my wife replied, looking out at the desert, trying to scan the entirety of it with a sweep of her head.

"It really is, isn't it?" he agreed.

87

Indian pictograph outside Fort Davis.

We turned around to face the inside of the cave. The manager remarked how he and his friends would come to this spot when they were teenagers to "hang out." "I'm really glad no one has left their garbage or graffiti here," he stated. Then he pointed to the reason for our visit. On two of the larger stones just inside the cave's mouth were paintings that date to the sixteenth century most likely, when the Spanish first brought the animals to the New World. One was blurred to my eye, and I had trouble making it out. Pointing closer, he said, "This one is a hunting scene. You see the horse and the rider?" Sure enough, with his explanation, we could make out the images he described. The other rock held an image much more vivid. It showed a figure, hands raised and perhaps riding or hunting. Although this image was clearer, the scene it was supposed to depict was just as cryptic as the other, at least for myself.

One year ago, on assignment in northwestern New Mexico, I, and the group of writers I was with, came upon several pictograms in the San Juan River basin. These illustrations were just as vivid as those we saw that morning in Fort Davis, if not more so. The difference was the style. The human figures in New Mexico were much fuller and proportioned individuals—triangle heads on plump, round bodies. The drawings in Fort Davis, thin enough to be stick figures, gave evidence of their age; these illustrations predated the New Mexican images by hundreds of years, if not a thousand. And while the New Mexican drawings represented a family, holding hands in a descending line of height, these in Fort Davis provided more base imagery (i.e., hunting, food acquisition)—the act of gathering sustenance, that activity that most separates us from the gods and brands us as the animals that we are. And here was our portrait, drawn by a hand that was simultaneously alien and familial. This picture was as much an image of the time period as it was an illustration of the entire human condition. Here, and in so many other locations throughout the Southwest, and indeed the world, these pictograms highlight our epic story. Here, our humanness is represented as a man alone, hands upraised in thanks, perhaps, for hunting success and illustrated on the other rock, the perfect representation of the hê—the rejoicing or praying man, the letter "E." Thousands of years and thousands of miles apart, from Knossos to Marfa, the same emotion produces the exact same sentiment, the same reaction to the environment.

We sat gazing at the landscape for a while longer before retracing our steps back to the car. Along the way, a large lizard, scaling the side of a tree we walked past, frightened my wife. The manager laughed. He was obviously more than familiar with the terrain.

The afternoon and its steadily increasing heat saw us driving back down Highway 17 toward Marfa. When we first encountered Marfa, several years ago, it was a small hamlet of a town, sleepy and slow. However, like Austin, Marfa has been discovered and has been filling up with artists and the like for these past few years. Much of the town's indigenous population has moved on, some displaced because the rise in property values exceeded their fixed incomes' revenue. Others have left because the area is simply not what it was. There is a constant stream of people nowadays that would have been unimaginable only a few short years ago. The few hotels and motels that have a history in the town now are remodeled, polished to a slick shine and charge a luxurious rate for the effort. The indigenous population has found that the influx of people has distilled a bitter drink. Like Austin, Marfa has become a mecca of sorts for the younger, hep crowd—think Kramer in a Stetson. However, there is still a majestic feel to the town—as if something very old, eclectic and colorful sleeps from late morning until early evening, waiting for the sun to set and the pagan fires to be lighted.

Marfa, Texas, like most of the towns out here, was founded on a single thought: get the railroad through. As with Alpine—which was earlier named "Murphyville" because Thomas O. Murphy owned the land that held the Burgess Water Hole—the Marfa area had ranches and water that were attractive to the railroad companies. The discovery of a small silver vein in the Chinati Mountains in the late nineteenth century meant that now the cattle as well as the silver needed to find a smooth, reliable track to market.

While the town was under construction—which is to say, while the railroad was laying its tracks through the territory—the town held the inglorious but utilitarian moniker of "Tank Town" due to the large water tank that filled the bellies of the steam engines. The switch to the name "Marfa" is, however, a point of contention.

Marfa, the story goes, was named for the Dostoyevsky character Marfa Ignatievna from *The Brothers Karamazov* by the wife of a railroad engineer as they steamed through the town back in 1882. It is said that this was the text she was reading at the time. This is the prevailing story and is, in fact, the one promulgated on the Marfa Chamber of Commerce website. However, the probability of this occurrence is very low. Dostoyevsky's novel, like much of Charles Dickens's work, was written in serial format, for the magazine *Russian Messenger*, with the final chapter published in November 1880. The first English translation did not appear until 1912, and it is doubtful that the engineer's wife could have had possession of the Russian magazine, much less been fluent in the language.

A much more reasonable suggestion is that the name "Marfa" is taken from the character Marfa Strogoff from the 1876 Jules Verne novel *Michel Strogoff*. This novel, considered one of Verne's finest, written originally in French, obtained a successful theatrical production in English that toured this country at that time. In fact, an entry in the *Galveston Daily News* dated from December 17, 1882, states that the name "Marfa" originates from this play. The article also goes on to state that other rail stops out in the same territory from the same time period took their names from this work.[23] Strange how the one rumor took root and has continued to thrive all these years when the fact that the Dostoyevsky book was not available at the time the railroad was making its initial trek through the region seems to trouble no one.

Whatever the origin of the name, Marfa has become a very unique entity out in the Trans-Pecos desert. As we drove into town that morning, the streets were nearly deserted. Of course, the focal point of the downtown area is the Presidio County Courthouse. As with so many older Texas towns, the courthouse is situated in the middle of the town square. The main street in Marfa, Highland Avenue, drives straight into the courthouse's entrance. The building itself, constructed in 1886 by architect Alfred Giles and remodeled in 2001, is a beautiful example of the Second Empire style of architecture. This style is characterized by tall, dual-sloped roofs with protruding windows called dormers, the high roof allowing for extra space inside the top floors. You are probably already familiar with the style. It is

Presidio County

Left: The water tower in downtown Marfa, Texas.

Below: Marfa, Texas, in the late nineteenth century. *Courtesy of the Clifford Casey Collection, Archives of the Big Bend.*

what the majority of the buildings in the older sections of Paris are modeled on. The Presidio County Courthouse is the perfect example of this style, in particular for the many dormers that decorate the outer edges of the roofs. Perhaps most striking of all, though, is the pink stucco exterior. Visible for several blocks in town, the unusual façade exhibits a stark contrast to the dusty, dry landscape. Highlighted by distinctive domes, the courthouse has been a tourist attraction all its own for decades.

Atop the central dome stands a statue of *Lady Justice*. In her right hand she holds a broken sword. The grip and cross guard intact, the blade is absent, although there is a contact slot for a blade that, maybe, has fallen away over the years. In the statue's left, clutching hand there is nothing. The story is that she should, and once did, hold a set of scales—the instrument of Justice. Local lore tells that, long ago, a criminal being led through town after conviction escaped his deputy's hold just long enough to shoot the scales from the statue's hand and shouted, "There is no Justice in this county!"—another tall tale in an area already stacked *this* high with such volumes. If the criminal really was that good a shot with a revolver, someone should have employed him in Buffalo Bill's Wild West Show.

Farther down Highland Avenue, we passed over the railroad tracks and had hoped to spend a few minutes inside the Marfa Book Company. A previous visit a couple of years before had been very nice. I had found an old Leon Russell CD in the stacks of music, and afterward we browsed a collection of art texts that were as complete and interesting as those in most

Present-day Marfa, Presidio County Courthouse.

libraries. On this day, my wife and I were rebuffed by the recession, again. The store was closed. We noticed, also, that the size of it was significantly less impressive than it had been. Whereas before, the store had occupied almost the entire block, now it was shrunk to about a third of its former size. To survive, the store had begun closing a couple of days a week, had sold the majority of its space and, we found the next day, even relinquished the coffee bar.

I'm not sure why I was so surprised by the turn of events, but I was. I was surprised that these hard times had exerted such a deleterious effort on a part of the country that has made a name for itself by not only withstanding such cruelties but also for stubbornly wading straight into them. In fact, the other businesses in town appeared to be just as we had last seen them. In any event, we found the store open the next morning. The older gentleman minding the bookstore confirmed our thoughts. The store had had to make necessary cutbacks that included not only the removal of the coffee bar but almost every ancillary product or superfluous bit of merchandise as well. As for the coffee and cookies that used to be available, he directed us to a new coffee and ice cream parlor just a couple of blocks west of the bookstore. Never one to miss an invitation to ice cream, even if that invitation is only a finger pointing in the right direction of the store, my wife and I soon found ourselves there, one eating ice cream and the other sipping an espresso. Both were delicious.

We splurged at lunch and ate at the Dairy Queen, a Texas tradition. (I had always thought that Dairy Queen was a Texas-only business. However, recently a friend told us that he sat at one in Minnesota. I felt betrayed for some reason.) It was a tradition that the local Border Patrol was also observing that afternoon. We stood in line behind a couple of olive-drab cloaked agents, one of whom had his green cap hanging from the butt of his 9mm pistol.

My wife, a Puerto Rican native, enjoys my sad attempts at speaking Spanish with her, so I oblige her when I feel up to it. That afternoon, I felt capable and spiced my speech with her *idioma*. For whatever reason, our conversation caught the attention of the Border Patrol agent in front of us. He, a young twentysomething, kept turning his head to inspect the strangers behind him. Even when he had placed his substantial order and gone to his table of confederates, he continued to turn and stare. Evidently we were foreign to his sharp experience.

After lunch, we drove back to the center of town and parked on the side of the Paisano Hotel. Much attention is given to this hotel, and it has become

The façade of the historic Paisano Hotel, Marfa, Texas.

a tourist attraction in and of itself. However, there is some justification for that; it is a grand building.

The Paisano was built by the architectural group Henry and Gustavus Trost in 1926. The Trost and Trost firm is responsible for hundreds of buildings in the state, but El Paso, their home office town, displays the majority of their work. Influenced by the work of contemporaries and colleagues like Louis Sullivan, William Gray Purcell and Frank Lloyd Wright, and inspired by the Transcendentalist writings of Ralph Waldo Emerson, Henry Trost's application of the Spanish Revival style is clearly evident at the Paisano. Built in an era when travel was a constant but relatively new enterprise, the Paisano was constructed with the functionality of the flow of traffic in mind. The rail station is just across the street and down a block. Indeed, the openness of the interior, which leads past the reception desk and toward the recessed restaurant and bar area, not only creates a familiar, inviting atmosphere but also hints at the physical aspect of motion. As Jay C. Henry wrote in his book *Architecture in Texas, 1895–1945*:

> *The interior of El Paisano, like all of Trost and Trost's small hotels, is executed in a generalized regional idiom of tiled floors and wainscots, exposed beam ceilings, roughcast plaster walls, and carved woodwork. Parabolic arches are used to frame main openings, and the parlor fireplace is carved with Meso-American ornament. Taken together with the Gage and El Capitan, and with the firm's other hotels in New Mexico and Arizona, El Paisano is a remarkable exercise in both functional planning and regional character.*

Normally, all of this attention to the building's architecture and age would be enough to qualify it for a star on any tourist's itinerary. However, the Paisano also has the distinction of having been the unofficial headquarters for the cast and crew of George Stevens's film *Giant* from 1956. The upstairs ballroom served as the director's impromptu screening room, and many of the actors had rooms at the hotel during filming. The Paisano touts the rooms in which Rock Hudson, Elizabeth Taylor and James Dean stayed while in town; however, the reality is that these rooms saw the stars infrequently. Most of them stayed in private residential homes around town.

The afternoon that we visited, we entered through the hotel's main door on Highland Avenue. The entrance is a walkway of a few shops, a couple dedicated to the film's legacy, and the Marfa Chamber of Commerce office. This leads on to the registration area, which is a wonderful, open reception.

The courtyard of the Paisano Hotel.

Standing at the registration desk, one can see the old staircase, the outdoor veranda and fountain and the passage to the bar and restaurant. The afternoon we stood in this vestibule, I had hoped to ask the receptionist a couple of questions about the hotel, but there was no one around. In fact, we walked around the entirety of the lobby, the restaurant and bar area and back again and saw not a single employee. We toured the outside fountain area and saw only one other person, an electrician walking back toward his truck parked on the side street.

We continued to pull in close to the cool, clean water of the fountain, catching a little spray and relief from the oppressive July heat. I also wanted to catch a scotch and water, but as it was only three o'clock in the afternoon, the bar, like so much connected with the hotel, lacked a human presence. I thought, having been a bartender all through college, that I could wander behind the bar, make my own drink and then leave payment under a glass somewhere. And I was just about to embark on this surreptitious task when my wife, in her usual didactic manner, reminded me of the adage that whomever you need is always unavailable just as those you hope to not see will certainly turn up in an instant.

She was right. If we had stood there waiting for some service at that bar, we would have waited through a couple of lunar cycles. But if I had journeyed behind the bar, the area would surely have filled with every employee past and present the instant I had bottle and glass in hand. Former owners of the property would take *that* moment for a meeting on the subject of Paisano remembrances. Those employees from yesteryear, buried out in the old cemetery, would have risen anew just to take part in my capture. The photographer of the *Big Bend Sentinel* newspaper, its offices just across the street, would most probably have come looking for his watch that he was sure he had left at the bar only the previous evening. He would arrive camera in hand, of course. My photo, the one of me standing trapped behind the Paisano bar, a bottle of scotch (oh, let it be good quality!) in one hand, an ice-filled glass in the other, mouth hanging open in apprehended surprise, would headline the *Sentinel* tomorrow. And then, because we live in Austin, the *Statesman* would have the same picture, but mercifully in the "Metro" section, tagged with the caption "Writer Caught Hot in Desert—Scotch Theft Scotched." After a couple of weeks, people here in town, when spying me at the grocery or on the street, would lift their arms in imitation, bulge their eyes and hang their mouths while yelping whatever single-syllable utterance they consider accompanied my crime. Of course, the Border Patrol will have stopped by the hotel to "just have a look around" at precisely the same moment that all of this is occurring.

I fed a few coins into the Coke machine instead and avoided the felony.

A few summers ago, while gathering research for a few articles on the Texas wine industry, we drove into the Texas Panhandle and then dropped

Downtown Marfa, 1930s. *Courtesy of the Archives of the Big Bend.*

down a few hundred miles south and west of that area. We began the journey in Lubbock and turned south toward Brownfield and Lamesa, and when we had reached the Midland-Odessa region, we turned and headed back north. Even though we were looking for wineries and vineyards (of which there are many in the state), I could not help but notice that every town, village, hamlet or coop had some sort of museum to a local, famous, almost famous or regionally famous icon. Texans, it seems, will display and hold testament to just about anything that reaches beyond the ordinary. Midland, for example, in addition to hosting the Presidential Museum and Leadership Library (which is actually a museum for George W. Bush and his family, who were residents of the area back when there was oil in the ground. The oil has been removed, and the Bushes left town when the oil did[24]), is also home to the Permian Basin Petroleum Museum. O'Donnell, Texas, boasts the Dan Blocker ("Hoss" on the TV show *Bonanza*) Museum. Monahans, Texas, holds claim to a Coca-Cola Museum inside of a Big Burger restaurant. So, when we came upon the Marfa–Presidio County Museum along Highway 90, aka West San Antonio Street, the sight of it did not seem out of place at all.

This repository of local artifact was bought by the town of Marfa in 1996 and opened as a museum a year later. The museum is a restored house built in 1883 by Don Juan Humphries (a more American name I do not believe I have ever read). It has been known since as the "Humphries Home." The purchase was allowed by the owner with the stipulation that the residence be used as a showcase for the town's antiquities and memorabilia. The museum houses one

The Marfa–Presidio County Museum.

of the nicest photograph collections in and of the area with more than two thousand prints and negatives. Items relating to the railroad, ranching, early settlers and Indians, mining and the military make up the collection. Because the other items are, for the most part, from the attics and barns and backyards of the residents, the artifacts are the real deal; these are the articles that helped mold, shape and create the territory. Just as the Annie Riggs Museum in Fort Stockton houses much of the material that has always existed in that area, the Marfa–Presidio County Museum is curator of those objects that have been at the sides of all of the territory's residents since the county was formed in the late nineteenth century. It is not the largest museum in the area, but Marfa has a story to tell nevertheless, and the illustrations are here.

My wife likes to relate how when she was a child and her family would fly between Puerto Rico and the Dominican Republic, everyone on the airplane would applaud and cheer when the plane touched down on the tarmac. Similarly, many years ago while I was attending Texas Tech University in Lubbock, while driving between Post and Denton, Texas, on Highway 380, I always noted that the closer I was to farmland and ranch land—which is to say, once I was past Jacksboro—the more frequently those trucks that I passed on that two-lane blacktop would wave as we passed each other. While we drove through this southwest section of the state, I was pleased to see that the custom has not been abandoned. The attitude of familiarity and neighborliness still exists for some of us, but evidently we have to escape the steel grip of the city to experience it again.

The evening after we had visited Marfa, my wife and I ate our dinner outside of the motel room on the porch. Soon we were sitting with a small group of people over by the pool area, the official locale for evening conversations. The pool, being near the street, offers a great view of the town, so it is, in a manner of speaking, the "front porch" of the motel. If this were Mayberry, Sheriff Taylor would sit here with his guitar after dinner.

It was here that, like applauding the landing plane or waving to the passing truck, we met and became friends with several other guests at the motel; all of us were just passing through the little city of Fort Davis and the Big Bend region of the state. Not a few evenings we sat outside listening to folks from all over Texas and beyond discussing everything from which rifle is best for hunting mountain goats to what type of shoe is best for elementary school–aged children.

There was the printer from Kerrville who, it turns out, also writes a weekly column for his town's daily newspaper. He and his family had taken several of the units off from one end of the strip of rooms. They were embracing their family reunion. Every morning, the group of them sat in the deck chairs along the walkway in front of the rooms, and every morning the printer would wave a *good morning*. More than once he ambled over to our area, and we would talk of the burden of writing regular columns for magazines or newspapers. At other times we talked about the anxiety of having a child in college. Because of the reunion and the fact that he and his family were enjoying their summer's vacation, they stayed longer at the motel than most travelers, and we were glad of it; their company made every morning a pleasure.

There was the concealed handgun instructor, with his chilling stories of working for Blackwater in Iraq. He spoke of death and killing with an insouciance that was frightening and then again with a sort of matter-of-factness that many soldiers obtain from repeated exposure to such violence. And because he lives along the Texas-Mexico border, he told other stories about leaving water and food on his property for the illegal immigrants who find themselves alone and far from home without any sustenance. "I won't deny water and some food to anyone that really needs it," he declared. "And man, sometimes those guys, after packing through the desert for a couple of days, really need it." He was traveling with his eight-year-old daughter. On a couple of afternoons, my wife braided the girl's hair while she played with her new wooden yo-yo. It was her first, so I showed her how to launch the thing from the palm of her hand over the back of her middle finger.

There were the two Alpine residents who rode up on their belching Harleys; they came to visit with the motel's manager and ended up leaving us all laughing out loud with their stories. One of these men related how he had been in Big Bend National Park during one of the heavy thunderstorms that the territory was receiving. Riding his motorcycle through a wooded spot of the park, he told of how, upon hearing a strange, rumbling sort of sound, he put the brakes on the bike and waited to see whether he might determine the source of the coming clamor. Soon, to everyone's amazement, he spoke of the crashing of enormous boulders and the tearing of trees straight out of the earth as the rush of some loosed waves from a breached dam or levee pushed and drove these huge blocks of rock and the heft of the trees right past him along a worn trail. He told us all how he had stood there, astride his bike, watching this magnificent display of nature literally let loose. We heard the tale of the rocks smashing apart while the shafts of trees rolled and tumbled among the shattering detritus of stones.

Highway 17 between Fort Davis and Marfa, "Old Marfa Highway."

"Do you have any idea what the odor of breaking boulders smells like?" he asked us all. Of course, none of us did. "It was the most amazing thing," he said, "the smell of the dirt inside of those rocks. It was clean, dusty, raw, primal—all at the same time." As he spoke, he lifted his hands to his face and breathed deeply, his eyes wide and bright. The expressions on the others' faces revealed that they, too, were captured by the story and could imagine what the sight may have been. "I'll never forget it," he said, and I am sure the rest of us will not, either.

Another man at the motel was with his four children, ages twenty-seven to eleven. The youngest was the only boy of the group, the others all being girls—young ladies, I should say, as the youngest of them were teenagers. There were six in all, and my wife and I took notice that a wife or mother was not a part of their company. This man was an oil field worker but, at forty-seven, had risen through the ranks and was now something of an executive with his firm. He spoke with authority and knowledge of the BP Gulf oil spill. He and I talked for some time about the disaster (for it can be described as nothing else) one morning, and everything that he said needed to be done was, in fact, what occurred in the coming weeks. He also described how crude, as it comes from the inner machinery of the earth, is different the world over; how Texas crude is of a different viscosity in west Texas as opposed to the Gulf regions; how oil from Alaska is an entirely different color and thickness; and how he has even seen crude that came so clear and light that it was possible to pour it straight into the older style of gasoline engines.

"That stuff'll make a monster outta' them older cars," he stated, adding, "That's what we used ta' put inta' our cars when I was a kid, and man, that oil'd burn so hot you could barely keep the car on the road!" He was soft-spoken, with a rich, east Texas accent that was at once endearing and soothing. The idea that he was a single parent to all of those children only further drew our affections toward him. His authority on the subject of oil derricks and rigs was matched only by his enthusiasm for hunting and, of course, his children.

Watching the daily influx of people was an exercise in sociology. The motel was an anthropological museum. Every race and age was represented at some time or another; the country was well represented. We met many of them. Some arrived to much fanfare and bluster—their own, of course, wasting little time before diving, screaming, into the pool. Others came and left unseen, covered by night's cloak, seen by no one except the motel's management. During our time at the motel, I was constantly amazed at the affability and pleasant dispositions of the people who worked there. There was a continual train of visitors, day and night. The motel's manager, garrulous and omnipresent, never rolled his eyes or uttered a single disparaging word in response to the phone's interminable ringing. The other employees went about their work with a smile that, as far as I could see, never left their faces. The first few days that we were in Fort Davis, this beatific attitude was surprising. Why was nearly everyone smiling and in a pleasant mood? After a few more days, we began to understand that the natural beauty of the place and its relatively small size contribute to a general sense of well-being. It is a contagion.

The following morning, we loaded up early. Our appointment at the Chinati Foundation was for ten o'clock, and I wanted to get there a little before the time.

The Chinati Foundation is actually a museum. It is also one of the most unusual museums in the state, perhaps the country. The property of the museum lies on a 340-acre tract of land just outside of Marfa that used to be an army base.

Created in 1911, Camp Albert, which was soon renamed Camp Marfa, was established to help defend the Rio Grande area and its residents from the daily and expanding threat of Pancho Villa and the other hostilities that accompanied the Mexican Revolution. Raids by Mexican bandits—and the general volatility that such violence, coupled with a porous international border, can cause—led to the United States government's installation of the military camp. The area had always been witness to a certain level of lawlessness, and this new danger demanded intervention on a federal scale.

Throughout the early years, Camp Marfa performed many duties. From biplane reconnaissance work along the border to offering troops large tracts of land on which to conduct military exercises, Camp Marfa stood at constant attention. Indeed, when Germany began encouraging and supporting the hostilities in Mexico, in an effort to divert American energies to the south rather than Europe, Camp Marfa saw that it was well positioned to defend from such aggressions.

In 1930, Camp Marfa was renamed Fort D.A. Russell in honor of General David Allen Russell, a Union officer killed during the Civil War in 1864. However, the renaming of the camp could not stave off the reality of the Great Depression, and the U.S. government initiated plans to close the fort in 1931. The Marfa Chamber of Commerce managed to hold off the closure for a couple of years, but in the end the camp was abandoned in January 1933.[25]

Fortunately for the community and the safety of the area, the camp was regarrisoned in 1935. Between this time and the fort's final closing in 1946, the troops built many of the structures seen today, in particular the artillery sheds and some of the barracks that today house much of the artwork at the museum. During these years, too, some of the camp was used to house German prisoners of war and another portion for officers' training. The camp was decommissioned in 1945 and by the following year was completely abandoned by the army. As with Fort Davis nearly three-quarters of a century earlier, the buildings and land were sold and inhabited by local residents.

In 1979, Minimalist artist Donald Judd, the *pater familias* of the Marfan art scene, bought a large section of the old camp, with much financial help coming from the Dia Art Foundation in New York City. One businessman I spoke with in Fort Stockton told me that he and several of his neighbors were not happy with the arrangement. His temperament was that Judd and Dia "stole that land" from those who had possession of it before. However, that was as far as his complaint went. He offered no proof or position for his opinion. Nevertheless, his willingness to relate this news to me only revealed what I had suspected about the region—that most of the people who live out here view the entire area as *theirs* and that the locals hold a very deep affinity for the land and, again, feel as though the whole of it is their responsibility to watch over and protect. It is a quality that I found deeply endearing.

After several years of construction, the museum was opened to the public in 1986. Since that time, the Chinati Foundation has become a fixture on the Marfan landscape. The museum draws an incredible number of visitors each year, offers internships for art students and also offers art classes for the community. In addition, the foundation hosts an annual "festival" every October that is open to all who would choose to come.

As was the case on our first visit to the foundation a few years before, when we arrived that morning there were only a couple of cars in the lot. And, as before, a very healthy calico cat stalked the area beneath the trees just outside the walls. When we entered, a group of three young women greeted us. When I told them my name, one who was seated behind the registration desk said, "Oh! Mr. Browne. Here." She reached under the desk and produced a small stack of papers. "These are for you." The papers were the foundation's press reports and clippings.

The museum conducts tours of its collection beginning about mid-morning and, because the tour is divided into two events, concludes by mid-afternoon. And although they accept walk-in visitors, the majority will have made a reservation. That morning, we waited a few minutes for a couple who had made a reservation before we began the walk through the foundation's artwork.

Both tours that we have taken through the museum have begun with the work of the foundation's founder, Minimalist artist Donald Judd. In the early 1970s, he purchased not only the 340 acres of Fort D.A. Russell but even a 45,000-acre ranch on the Rio Grande as well.

Judd had moved to Texas in order to calm an inner displeasure with the art scene in New York. He also sought a more peaceful atmosphere and a larger, empty canvas with which to begin work on permanent art installations, the art's permanency within a space being his prime goal. Judd felt that art being moved from one museum to another and being shifted from one environment to another disparaged the work, so he explored the possibilities of constructing his pieces in an environment where the work would reside perpetually on a canvas of his choosing. Further, Judd envisioned this new space, Fort Russell, as needing more work to complete the scope of his vision. To accomplish this, he asked fellow artists such as Carl Andre, Dan Flavin, Ilya Kabakov, John Wesley and John Chamberlain, among others, to contribute work; the works of these other artists are placed throughout the old army base. Indeed, most were given their own buildings to work with, and like Judd's work, all are permanent installments at the site.

The tour first walks visitors outside to have a look at Judd's *15 Untitled Works in Concrete*. These are large concrete blocks that lie in the tall grass out in a distant area of the old army base. The juxtaposition of the work against the desert sky and grassy landscape is sublime. The guide told us that after the tour proper was completed, we could feel free to walk out to these blocks to have a closer inspection. My wife and I considered this for a while, but the news that the grounds crew had recently killed a rattlesnake nearby deterred our plan.

Judd's *100 Untitled Works in Mill Aluminum* are also prominently displayed in the front artillery sheds. These structures were refurbished in the early 1980s to include large, wall-sized windows that allow the sun to reflect on and off the aluminum. The effect is stunning, and again the contrast between the work and the dry, almost sterile atmosphere of the old sheds is dramatic.

Dan Flavin, an artist famous for his work with light, light sources and the colors emitted, was given several of the old barracks with which to work. These U-shaped block buildings are the perfect environment for the elongated, colored neon bulbs with which he chose to work. The area from the door leading toward the back, where the lights glow, is vacant and sleek. The neon bulbs hum their energy down the walkway and radiate color from their central location at the juncture of the U in each barrack.

During our walk among these barracks, we met a couple from Los Angeles who had stopped in Marfa on their drive to Dallas, where a new job waited for one of them. One of the two men was a native Texan and had seen the museum before. His partner was new to the state and Marfa alike. He was enthralled that such an exhibit should be located in a west Texas desert. "This is so cool!" he said as he entered each new building and encountered a new series of colors emanating from the back. His partner simply smiled knowingly. My wife took several pictures for them as they stood in front of the fluorescent lights, bulbs and men alike glowing with satisfaction.

Ingólfur Arnarsson's space is a quintessential example of the Minimalist style. The rectangular room is, save the cement floor, bone white throughout, with blank, pale gray canvases spaced equally along the walls. As I've written elsewhere, the effect is almost ethereal, and the visitor's presence within the space appears as an intrusion on the quiet perfection—phantasms interloping in a space that is complete without their company.

One of the museum's most popular works is that of Russian artist Ilya Kabakov. His *School No. 6* is a representation of an abandoned Soviet-era schoolhouse. Complete with waste wood beams and strewn papers, the interior suggests a rapid retreat from some unknown threat. The items Kabakov chose to illustrate his childhood—academic memories, musical instruments, biology specimens, report cards, assorted assignments and a

Untitled Works 1991–1992 by Ingólfur Arnarsson, Chinati Foundation Museum. *Courtesy of the artist.*

portrait of Lenin, all covered in dust and neglect—serve to intimate a sort of stilted normalcy. Indeed, each time we have visited, the tour guides have admonished visitors to be careful to not touch anything—"Even the dust is where the artist wants it to be."

The tour takes a break after a couple of hours and reconvenes in a different building in downtown Marfa to show the works of John Chamberlain. These works—old, mangled car parts soldered together and painted with bright color—are recognizable to most of us over forty years old as they were much publicized in art history texts during our college years.

When the tour was completed, we met with one of the foundation's directors, Ann Nafziger. Ms. Nafziger had arranged the tour for us that day, and we wanted to thank her for all of her help. As we spoke, my wife mentioned that for a few years we had always passed a large white building in the residential neighborhood leading to the Chinati Foundation and that we never had been able to find out what the structure was. It is an unusual thing because the façade is of a castle, of sorts, with turrets and cornices. It is somewhat out of place, even in the wonderland that is west Texas. Ms. Nafziger laughed and related that the building is the old fort's pool. Though out of service now, she told us that behind the "castle's" walls is a full, large pool that has not been used in many years. The three of us had the same idea to restore the thing and open it to the public. Maybe someone will seize the thought and follow through. On a typical July afternoon in west Texas, a pool could make a wonderful stop for the museum's tour.

A few years ago, when writing about this subject for another magazine, my wife and I left the Chinati Foundation and headed directly west out of town

Interior of *School No. 6* by Ilya Kabakov, Chinati Foundation Museum. *Courtesy of the artist.*

on Highway 90 for Valentine, Texas. John Troesser, editor of *Texas Escapes* magazine, had told me about another art installation that was an absolute necessity for any article about the art scene in this part of the country.

We had never stopped in Valentine before. On our first time through, we had delayed lunch with the thought that we would grab something in Valentine as we passed through. Let me tell you, if you're planning on grabbing anything to eat in Valentine, Texas, you better know someone there, call them and ask them to put the coffee on, because there is not a public restaurant of any sort in the community. The only meal you are going to get is if someone you are familiar with makes you something after you arrive. Or, of course, you can always bring your lunch with you and just eat it there. But, again, you may want to make the acquaintance of a local, as there is no park, rest stop or intersection where you could relax, inconspicuous, and enjoy a tepid meal.

This time we did stop in Valentine, not for food but rather because my wife had read something interesting about the town. We stopped at the only building in town at which one can stop uninvited, the post office.

The Valentine city limit. Always more heart than *gente*.

Postmaster Maria Elena Carrasco, Valentine, Texas.

The Valentine Post Office has become something of an international celebrity over the years for its business of placing a special Valentine's stamp on cards and letters each Valentine's Day. Postmaster Maria Elena Carrasco, each new school year, visits the Valentine school and conducts a contest among the students for the next season's Valentine's image. They have been offering these special postal stamps for a number of years now, dating back to the 1980s, and each year's production is as original and unique as the town from which it originates. Of the entire process, Ms. Carrasco stated, "To me, it's not so much about the romance and candy and flowers and all that advertisement but rather about the love between a grandmother and her granddaughter or a mother and her son or an uncle and his nephew. It's about God's love for all of us. So, in a way, when I mail those cards, I'm spreading God's love."

We looked through the collection of past stamps, and Ms. Carrasco and my wife held a discussion in Spanish for a few minutes. As usual, I stood nearby, smiling stupidly and listening for my name.

When we left the post office that morning, we drove into the town of Valentine to have a look around. There had been a construction team working along the highway when we entered, and I wanted to see what the level of progress was in the area. It was minimal, judging by the appearance of the town back off the highway. The school was clearly the focal point of the community and, indeed, had been a frequent topic of Ms. Carrasco's talk.

Presidio County

We left Valentine and headed out farther west on the highway. Driving another few miles, we came upon that thing that had brought us out this way, initially, four years before: the *Prada Marfa*. One of the most unusual and striking art installations I have ever seen is standing in the west Texas desert, alone and daily bearing the burden of the brutal Texas weather and passing remarks. The work is a permanent art installation that has the semblance of being an outlet of the famous Italian boutique. Designed and erected by Berlin-based artists Michael Elmgreen and Ingar Dragset, the work contains six handbags and fourteen right shoes, hand picked by Miuccia Prada herself. I cannot be sure, but I think that a few of the purses were different from the last time we were out there.

The small building has the sad distinction of being the recipient of not only much cynical commentary but also a couple of black eyes.

Formally "opened" in 2005, vandals waited all of three days before breaking down the door and running off with all of the Prada materials (what anyone would want with fourteen right shoes is anyone's guess). Because the genre of the piece—referred to generally as "Architectural Land Art" or "Earth Art"—dictates that the materials used be natural, the original idea was for the structure to erode back into the west Texas desert with time. Indeed, this is a major component of most Earth Art projects (i.e., that the works evolve and decay over time just as any other object in nature would). Think of the famous *Spiral Jetty* work by Robert Smithson in the Great Salt Lake in Utah. Made from the earth and black basalt rocks of the area, the spiral will, over time, completely disappear (although there is an effort today

Prada Marfa. Courtesy of Ballroom Marfa.

to preserve and protect the work, as is, from oil and gas exploration in the area). In fact, many of these Earth Art projects exist today only through photographs or some other external, secondary evidence.

Prada Marfa still stands today, although it bears the bruises of past abuse. Walking to the side of the building, the imprint of the word "dumb" is still visible under the sandblasting that was used to clean the paint from the wall. (When I see this erasure, I always wonder if the word is a work of fiction or autobiography.) The structure's construction was also altered to be stronger and longer lasting in order to protect against further abuses. However, in the process, the reconstruction efforts have disparaged the original intentions—the glass is now plexiglass, and the purses are bottomless so that cameras could be placed inside. The exterior also has cameras placed strategically to capture would-be vandals. It is a sad indictment on ourselves that works of art, church naves, archaeological sites and more need be policed and protected from this sort of random and pointless destruction.

Because our calendar called for days, and nights, away from the Marfa area for the remainder of our trip, we decided to drive back to town that evening to try and catch a glimpse of the mysterious Marfa Lights.

You may have heard of these phenomena, those pulsating, flashing entities that have been described as everything from swamp gas to the dancing spirits of Apache warriors. These illuminations have astounded thousands for centuries, but the first recorded sighting comes, of course, from a Marfan ranch hand, Robert Ellison, in 1883. Ellison and his comrades saw the lights one evening while out in the desert with their herd. Thinking that the lights were approaching Apache Indians, Ellison and his crew doused their own fires to avoid detection.

Throughout the years, many people have tried to find the lights' sources, but with no success. Pilots training at the Marfa Air Field during World War II even tried to discover the lights' origins by flying over the area, but they, too, found nothing. There are even stories of the lights being beneficent—of leading people stranded in blizzards to a cave's safety or of enveloping the lost in a green, phosphorescent glow and leading them to terra cognita. Nowadays, efforts to find sources have all but ceased, and the community has built a viewing area for the public to watch the phenomena each clear night.

We arrived at this viewing area a little after nine o'clock in the evening and found that the site was already full of visitors. After several minutes of staring out into the desert, some of the folks around us began to declare that they could see the lights. While we could see a single light off in the distance, it was clear that this one was the flood lamp to some barn or storage building. However, after a few more minutes, a series of twinkling lights began to appear in the distance. At first there were three of these. They held the appearance of single headlamps except that they held a triangular formation and, after a moment of holding this shape, began to drift apart from one another. Soon, one of the three lights disappeared, only to reappear a moment later in a different position. After this event, the other two began to float around each other, moving apart and coming back together at an irregular interval—an ethereal dance to be sure.

The crowd was giddy with excitement and restless with the possibility of contact with another world. There were the usual pronouncements of machismo intended to dispel fears and guard against the potential embarrassment that the unknown can oftentimes bring. "I'll betcha' them lights is just some kid with a Halogen lamp sittin' out there!"—spoken loud enough for all to hear in the evening's darkness. "If those lights get anywhere near me, I'm gonna' pull my cellphone on 'em!" Still not too sure what that one was supposed to mean. It was a running commentary about the lights themselves and the effects they were having on each individual as we all sat out there in the Texas desert, in the dark, and waited and wondered just what was going on out in the distance.

"Didja' see that? Oh my! There it is again!"

"Were those lights there a second ago? I don't remember."

"There it is again! Is that a Marfa Light?"

"Oh, that's just the new highway over there. The Marfa Lights always show up over there, more to the left." The guy points, and all who can actually see his hand look in that direction.

"I thought the lights were supposed to be green or somethin'.'"

"Now, *those* lights weren't there just a minute ago. Did ya' see that one? Where in the world are those coming from? Does anyone know where these are supposed to be comin' from?"

"Is that them over there? What are they supposed ta' look like?"

And so on and so on. The group of us stayed about an hour and a half. Those with children packed it up sooner than the others, and when my wife and I took our leave of the Observation Center, only a couple who were searching for each other's inner light more than any desert anomaly was left to take note of the desert's wonders.

6.

NORTH-CENTRAL JEFF DAVIS COUNTY

The land is literally reaching for the stars. It is as if, in an effort to be closer to the creator and the heavens, the ground itself stretches upward, a suppliant offering praise and obeisance. Extending farther, an arm from the ground's body, a mountain grasps at sky and clouds. This is Fort Davis, the "mile high" town, and the mountain is Mount Locke, just northwest of the community. If you were of a mind to establish an astronomical observatory in Texas, this location would call to you for recognition. And it did.

In February 1926 a "slightly eccentric prosperous North Texas banker, William Johnson McDonald," died. McDonald's will bequeathed hundreds of thousands of dollars to his various nephews and nieces (he was a lifelong bachelor). Strangely, he wanted the remainder to go to the University of Texas at Austin for the construction of an astronomical observatory, which he wanted named for himself. The unusual request made McDonald's relatives see stars. Because the amount left, after the relatives' portions were distributed, was substantial, these same relatives decided that clearly Uncle Bill was of an unsound mind. However, Uncle Bill was also a voracious reader of all things science and art related. This was to be his legacy to himself, his way of demonstrating that he had held interests in life other than real estate. In fact, McDonald "used to tell his barber that someday a telescope would be constructed that would enable astronomers to see the gold-paved streets of New Jerusalem."[26]

The nieces and nephews cared little for Uncle Bill's academic pursuits or his religious visions. The monies were contested for several years in Texas courts. As Dr. David Evans wrote, McDonald's will "set the cat among the legal pigeons in Texas."[27] After several court appearances, the money decided that it had seen enough of lawyers and their constant dickering and settled, in 1929, into the stalwart, capable hands of the university to the astronomical sum of $840,000. This was, at the time, an amount sufficient for the construction of just such an observatory. However, as former observatory director Harlan Smith wrote, "The McDonald gift came to an institution, indeed to a state, with no practicing astronomers."[28] Someone was going to have to go find somebody to operate the place after it was built. The partner came from an unlikely source.

The year 1932 was a watershed one for the McDonald Observatory. That year, an internationally recognized astronomer by the name of Otto Struve became director of the Yerkes Observatory at Williams Bay, Wisconsin. Also that year, the University of Texas signed a proposal with the University of Chicago, a collaboration wherein the Texas university would build the observatory and the Chicago university would operate the site "while Texas got its astronomical act together."[29] What do these two items have in common? The University of Chicago operates the Yerkes Observatory. Soon, Director Struve would come to Fort Davis to set things to right. Again, as Harlan Smith observed:

> *By this time Otto Struve had been effectively the Director at Yerkes, and knew of the McDonald bequest. With enthusiastic support from his colleagues, George Van Biesbroeck, he began to lay plans for an inter-university collaboration wherein Chicago would provide astronomers and Texas, the money to build a joint observatory. In November, 1932, a 30-year contract to that effect was signed.*

There are within the history of the observatory many wondrous stories about the enormous mirrors created for use inside the telescope's turret. The creation, shaping, edging, handling, polishing and preservation of a piece of Pyrex glass with a diameter of eighty-two inches were all high drama for those involved. That it took two full days to get the thing from the train station in Alpine up onto the mountain is a story unto itself. That some vainglorious, disgruntled employee tried to drill it full of holes with a handgun in 1970 is still an occult topic at the observatory. (I suppose the idea is to not give any future employees silly ideas.) Suffice it to say that the thing is a work of art in the strictest sense and that those whose job it is to see to its care and handling take that responsibility very seriously.

McDonald Observatory under construction. *Courtesy of the Clifford Casey Collection, Archives of the Big Bend.*

The underside of a telescope, McDonald Observatory.

Viewing time with the machine is also at a premium and an equally serious topic. The University of Chicago relinquished control of the observatory in 1962 at the end of the thirty-year contract. Since that time, even though the transition has been gradual, the University of Texas has obtained almost exclusive rights to the facilities—and the facilities nowadays are as expansive as the west Texas desert. Indeed, the main issues most days at the observatory are who, when and for how long any single organization or single astronomer has possession of the telescopes. Time with the equipment is precious. Again, Smith commented that "until 1969, the two universities continued to share telescope time relatively equally."[30] One day that my wife and I visited, the tour guide, a young female student from the University of Texas at Austin, commented that visiting astronomers take their chances with the weather when making reservation time with the telescopes.

If it rains or is overcast on their assigned day, it is unfortunate that they will need to reschedule far into the future; they have to get back in line, as it were. There are always many more waiting.

To date, there are four primary telescopes at the McDonald Observatory. The eighty-two-inch lens is now named the Otto Struve Telescope. Indeed, the lens's design was by Otto Struve, and it was he who "accepted" the mirror, all 4,200 pounds of it, in 1938 after it had been poured by the Corning Corporation in Pennsylvania in 1933.

North-Central Jeff Davis County

The newest telescope on the mountain is the Hobby-Eberly Telescope, or HET. With construction begun in 1994, the telescope began its work in 1997. This telescope is the current pride of the complex, with ninety-one hexagonal segments that together offer a field of seventy-eight square meters. Each segment is "one meter side to side and weighs 250 pounds." The telescope's primary function is "to gather a very large amount of light, specifically for spectroscopy."[31] The young lady who was our guide that morning mentioned that the telescope was involved in astronomers' attempts to find dark energy. One can only surmise that spectroscopy has something to do with that effort.

These great telescopes reside atop Mounts Locke and Fowlkes, just outside of Fort Davis, the original eighty-two-inch situated on Locke and the new HET on the latter, respectively. Because most everyone in the Fort Davis area is mindful and respectful of the observatory's need for absolute darkness, the land in and around town has purposefully—and blessedly, in this age of development—been left in its natural state. As such, when driving through the area, these blond domes punctuate the mountain's verdant appearance with as much drama as the activity within, but they are as fragile as eggs in tall grass. If you drive down State Street, the main avenue in Fort Davis, after ten o'clock in the evening, you'll notice that all of the lights are either dimmed or extinguished, the deliberate darkness offering from a humble village.

In 1932, Violet Locke McIvor donated two hundred acres to the University of Texas for the placement of the observatory. She, of course, was asked for the land after several astronomers had scoured the state for a suitable location as free of artificial light as possible. Again, as Otto Struve observed:

> *The region of the Davis Mountains definitely presented the best possibilities within the state of Texas and promised to give conditions but slightly, if at all, inferior to those in Arizona and on the Pacific Coast.*
> *The number of clear, or partly clear nights per year is between 290 and 300. There are no wholly clear summer months, as in California, but the winters are probably better. The seeing is often very good, and the improvement over conditions at Yerkes is very marked.*[32]

The tall hill was renamed Mount Locke, from the ranch name U-Up U-Down, in honor of Ms. McIvor's grandfather, Scott Locke, a New Hampshire rancher who had bought the 40,000-acre spread in 1882. He moved his family to Texas back then, and the family has been on the land ever since. However, not dissimilar to the Stillwell Ranch, the Lockes have watched reluctantly as most of the acreage has been sold off over the years to pay for taxes. Today there are about 6,800 left for the family, and even this is in dispute, since Violet Locke's son signed over a great deal of the property to The Nature Conservancy (TNC) group. This is another story but one that many old Texas ranchers are telling with greater frequency.

Soon thereafter, four hundred more acres were acquired from the Fowlkes ranch, and this, in tandem with the Lockes' land, has allowed the observatory to expand over the years. The facilities now include a large new Visitor's Center, quarters for the employees and visiting astronomers and even a recreation area for the employees.

Ms. Rebecca Johnson, the McDonald Observatory's press officer, with an office in Austin at the university, secured a couple of passes to one of the biweekly "Star Parties" for my wife and me. My ego received a great and needed boost when we arrived at the information booth. A young woman behind the counter, having been given news of our arrival, smiled and said, "Oh, Mr. Browne! You're the one writing the book. Good to see you both. We've been expecting you!" Obviously, Ms. Johnson's good nature extended far beyond the confines of her Austin office.

Any visit to this part of the state should include a Star Party. These events are absolutely extraordinary, and any opportunity to attend should not be passed over.

Beginning just at dusk, the audience is first taken into a theater and shown a brief film about the history and ongoing research of the observatory. Afterward, now outdoors, the group ascends a winding path that leads to an amphitheater, of sorts, where one of the observatory's astronomers delivers a talk on the stars and planets overhead, replete with a green laser pointer for indicating the constellations above. The information is disseminated skillfully and oftentimes humorously. The subject matter is as vast as the skies above, so the lecture is kept focused on the constellations that are apparent in the season, with an emphasis on the changes that have occurred over the centuries (i.e., which star clusters and focal points have changed as the result of Earth's rotating axis and general position in the galaxy). We also had the opportunity to witness several satellites sailing overhead, an occurrence that we would have missed had the astronomer not literally pointed them out to us with his shimmering green beam.

The last segment of the Star Party is the viewing of the moon and a few planets through smaller telescopes that the observatory sets out. "Smaller" is, perhaps, not the right word and is relative only within the scope of the other telescopes on site. A couple of these smaller telescopes are so *small* as to require not only their own viewing facility but also stepladders to reach the oculus, or eyepiece. The lines to see each of these wonders were long. However, they were definitely worth the wait. The chance to view the surface of the moon so close and so clear was fantastic. Likewise, being able to witness Saturn girded by its famous rings was an experience not likely to be forgotten any time soon.

My wife and I queued up at the telescope pointed at Saturn. The line here, as at each, was about twenty-five persons long. Here was a young man, with a few small children in tow, being dogged by one of his daughters, all of six years old.

"Daddy! Daddy! When can I see? Pick me up! I want to see!" She was frantic, and the whole group of us became willing to wait her turn just to mollify her earnestness and tears. Her father, on the other hand, told a different story. He told her his story in a *forte voce* meant for us all, meant to both excuse and explain his family's time at the eyepiece:

"The last time I was here, twenty years ago, my father told me that I wouldn't understand what I was looking at and never let me have a turn at the telescopes. I've regretted it ever since. I've thought about that night for twenty years. Tonight, I'm taking my turn dammit! I've waited twenty years for this chance to come back around, and I'm not going to miss it again." And then, to his daughter: "Now look here. You'll get your turn. I'll pick you up and hold you to the finder, but right now, I'm gonna' take my chance, finally!" And with that, he stepped up the few metal stairs and peered, for the first time, upon Saturn and its luminous, encircling rings that had waited those twenty years just for his gaze. "Oh my God!" he declared as much to himself as to his family. "This is amazing!" He stood on the platform for a moment or two longer than the protocol set by those before, but none of us cared.

As he stepped down to reach for his daughter, those of us in the viewing area began to applaud his effort and determination. We were all glad that he had finally had this vision realized. He bowed his head and raised a quieting hand. He knelt down, picked his daughter up in one arm and held her close to the telescope's eye.

"There, baby. Do you see it?" In her excitement, she was left only with the ability to parrot her father: "Oh my God! That's amazing!" He held her to the telescope while she grasped at the sides of the viewer with both hands, trying to pull the image in closer as if nursing on the celestial image. This memory would be twenty years of substance and animation in its retelling—for father and daughter alike.

The HET
Telescope atop
Mount Fowlkes.

The McDonald Observatory's tour is, when taken properly, a two-day event. The first, the Star Party, should be followed the next morning by a return visit to tour the areas that house the telescopes. As on the previous night, the morning's procedure was to return to the theater for a video on the *Star Date* radio program and then a real-time viewing of the sun's surface. Unfortunately, the skies would not permit this that day. It was cloudy. There was more trouble from the tropical depressions that continued to roll across the state. In order to compensate for the sun's obscurity, the observatory's employee, a young astronomy student from the University of Texas at Austin, showed a recent video image of the sun. Even with a week-old video on a projection screen, the sun's power and violence were evident. It was quite a show.

The HET and Harlan Smith Telescopes are "up the hill" from the Visitor's Center. It is a short, steep drive up to the top. And the view from the summit of Mount Locke is gorgeous.

After driving to the top of Mount Locke, the tour guide left us standing outside along the railing while she checked on something indoors. The wind that morning was a more potent lift than any cup of coffee could ever hope to be. Those who had worn shorts and sandals for the day were suddenly second-guessing their decision as the wind whipped and chirled around us. Hair was mussed, and caps were tossed, but all of us were more enthralled with the view than with any vanity. Again, because of the heavy and continuous rains that the area had been experiencing, the mountains and valleys produced a vista that could rival any telescopic view of a distant land.

Because Mount Locke has an altitude of 6,800 feet, the range of vision around an area already a "mile high" is astounding. Standing near and then above clouds gray and heavy with rain is an experience unmatched even by the window seat on an airplane. No need to try and reach out to touch these billowing wafts of vapor; we were literally standing inside of them. We *were* them to anyone down in the valley looking up our way that morning.

The guide returned and led us up a winding flight of stairs to the main room of the Harlan Smith Telescope. The magnitude and simple enormity of the telescope is difficult to explain. Just as with those twenty-seven-thousand-gallon vats of wine at the Ste. Genevieve winery, the size of the machine is astounding. The "tube," or the telescope proper, is thirty-two feet in length, with a circumference of twelve feet. The weight of the tube is an astronomical 160 tons. The base of the device held, of course, many buttons, wires, switches and knobs. The whole machine was operated from a computer that sat on a table off to the side. The huge dome of the roof was also operated from this same computer station.

The guide, after manipulating some buttons and keys, caused the entire dome's ceiling to rotate, an activity that produced as many *oohs* and *ahhs* from the crowd as movement in the roof. The great shell creaked and roared like some massive robot coming to life, a well-oiled, titanic tin man reawakened. This is hardly an exaggeration, since the dome weighs in at 435 tons—870,000 pounds of steel, determination and vision. We were all startled to attention as the entire dome began to twist to the left. For some, finding a stationary focal point on the ground was necessary to offset the vertigo of the room becoming unscrewed. Of course, the guide allowed one of the children in the group to push the red "GO" button.

Another series of buttons allows for the floor, that portion sustaining the telescope, to swivel toward the opening in the ceiling. Looking around the room at our little class, I noticed that, with all the spinning of parts, machinery and space, we had all, somewhat unconsciously, sucked up against whatever wall or railing was available, as if we were waiting for some ride at the fair to begin.

The next, and final, stage of the morning's tour was a stop at the HET, the Hobby-Eberly Telescope. Because of the fragility of this machine, most tourists have to visit this telescope

Mount Locke adorned with telescopes.

119

from the other side of a viewing glass. The work is still very impressive. The ninety-one glittering, hexagonal components of the "mirror," permanently perched at a fifty-five-degree angle, really do resemble "bug eyes," as a child commented. The guide described the observatory's search for the existence of dark matter, and at the end of her talk I still wouldn't recognize the stuff if I walked straight through it.

While we gawked at the marvel of the mirror, we were told about the delicate transportation of each hexagonal piece, how each piece was inlaid by hand and how, on a regular schedule, each mirror is cleaned with "dry ice snow."

The tour ended where it had begun, at the Visitor's Center. We noticed that several of those from our group headed to the snack bar or the gift shop, so we took advantage and headed to the parking lot to avoid the rush of cars. It might not be surprising that the drive back to Fort Davis in the late morning, through the Davis Mountains, was an extraordinary event.

A couple of meandering, serpentine miles south of the observatory, Highway 118 flickers past Davis Mountains State Park. Opened for public use in the 1930s, much of the park was constructed and then improved upon by the Civilian Conservation Corps during Roosevelt's reconstruction efforts. And those efforts, all 2,708 acres of them, are manifold and diverse.

By the simple fact of the park's placement within one of the most beautiful areas of the state, it has become one of the state's favorites for those wishing to camp, hike and explore. However, all of the park's enjoyment is not found solely outdoors.

Inside the park is the Indian Lodge. Built in the 1930s, also by the CCC, and opened in 1939, this lodge has been "voted the #1 accommodation in Texas by readers of Texas Highways Magazine in 1992."[33] Little has changed to alter opinion since that time, and the accommodations are some of the best in the entire state. When considering that, in addition to the extraordinary

The entrance to Davis Mountains State Park.

lodging, there are numerous deer, goats, javelina, antelopes, black bears and even mountain lions in the area and that the morning's bird-watching is second only to the evening's stargazing, it is a mystery why tourists would stay anywhere else when visiting the area. The state's highway department has also graciously supplied seventy-two miles of "scenic loop" (State Highway 166) that wind, bend, ascend and descend around and through the Davis Mountains. A single day's activity that might involve touring the area via this loop with a terminus at the Indian Lodge, and all that this could entail, would make for an extraordinary day steeped in all things Texas.

We had stayed in the Fort Davis area, we figured, just long enough. We had lived in the same motel room for a little more than two weeks, a stay that saw us, at first, happily greeted and treated as guests, and then progressed into a sort of lazy familiarity; finally, we became the dinner guests who had, perhaps, overstayed their invitation.

We became familiars to the town's lone loner, a man who, although not homeless, took his meals in the alley behind the store and spent his afternoons camped in a vacant lot across the street from the motel sitting on the ground and listening to his music from age-old headphones. When I was told that a trust fund sustains him, I was surprised. When I learned that he holds an advanced degree in mathematics, I was not as amazed. As a local resident put it, "It's always the math guys."

We had stayed in the town long enough to be on first-name basis with some of the motel's staff and to recognize their schedules just as surely as they had come to know ours. We had stayed long enough that a couple of chairs by the pool expected our presence each night after supper. We had stayed long enough to receive not quite pleasant glances from the frustrated artist working in the neighboring convenience store. We had driven the streets, had walked the sidewalks, had spent hours in the public laundromat, had passed hours in the library and even knew on which aisle the cereal was in the local grocery. In short, I thought we had filled our Fort Davis agenda and could pack it in and move on. I was wrong.

About four miles south from Fort Davis on Highway 118, just past the World's Greatest Rest Area, is the Chihuahuan Desert Nature Center. Having lived in Austin for the past several years, I imagined that I had seen the best of the nature center world. Not until you have walked the five miles of trails at the Chihuahuan Desert Nature Center can you truly say that you have experienced such a place. Without question this is one of the finest examples of a nature conservatory in the country.

Greenhouse, Chihuahuan Desert Nature Center and Botanical Gardens. The greenhouse is at the back of the "Butterfly Trail," housing hundreds of cacti species.

At 507 acres, this center is complete with just about every type of flora—cacti and succulents—that one could hope to see represented. The list of the hundreds of plants and flowers is much too extensive to begin here. Nevertheless, the gathering of flowers, trees, cacti and shrubs here is a wondrous congregation.

For the record, let me state that I am inherently averse to mission statements. They have always struck me as pretentious and almost pointless. "Action not words" is a phrase for which I have more affinity. In my experience, mission statements are often not the didactic, explanatory treatises that an organization offers to an ignorant populace but rather, frequently, are the stately regulations and aspirations that an organization directs at its employees and associates as a reminder to try and accomplish those tasks that are often ignored or left undone. This is not the case with the Chihuahuan Desert Nature Center. The mission statement at the center is this:

> *The mission of the Chihuahuan Desert Research Institute is to promote public awareness, appreciation, and concern for the natural diversity of the Chihuahuan Desert region through research and education.*[34]

Notice the focus is on public education. The center's website is an extensive, informative, user-friendly site that is obviously designed to promote the nature center as clearly as possible to a public that may be unfamiliar. The site makes frequent and steady mention of symposia, workshops, field trips and lectures. It also announces a program for elementary school–aged children called the Chihuahuan Desert Field School. In addition, the center offers scholarships and grants for continuing education. In all, the center is dedicated to the natural desert environment. A walk through the premises illustrates this dedication with a blooming flower's attraction.

The morning my wife and I visited the center, we were greeted by a woman who told us that she was a volunteer, a retired state employee who had, initially, taken this job because "it [was] close to home and the hours were flexible." She also stated that she has remained at the center for close to a decade because she has become enthralled with the center's commitment to preservation and conservation efforts. She was obviously proud to be associated with the place.

She handed us the site's hiking map, explained where the individual trails were and made a special comment on one trail, the Outside Loop Trail, that extends onto the top of the William's Overlook, the highest point within the park. The trails are evaluated from easy to moderate to difficult in reference to the terrain and length. We opted for the Hummingbird and Butterfly Trail, which, although it is graded as "easy," we took mainly because I had worn my sandals that morning instead of a pair of hiking shoes. Really.

The trail in the morning's sun was stunning. The light penetrated through the bushes and trees, illuminating them to the point of majesty. The flowers' blooms glowed under this soft fire, while the birds, invisible within the foliage, sang their contented songs. This trail winds slowly uphill and culminates at the Cactus and Succulent Collection. This collection is housed in a large greenhouse midway along the Hummingbird Trail. As the center's website explains, there are more than two hundred species of these plants in the collection, and although the center is open year round, March and April are highlighted as those months when many of these are in bloom.

I'll admit that a visit to a nature center was not a trip that I was eagerly anticipating. The idea of it, before we visited, left me with the same feeling I had as a child in Lubbock when our mother would despotically command us to accompany her to the fabric store. All look, no touch, no fun. However, after our visit I am eager to return, to hike the trails we did not, to see the terrain from the vistas we missed and to experience again this remarkable section of the desert.

Chihuahuan Desert Nature Center and Botanical Gardens. The entrance is off SH 118.

7.

SOUTHWEST BREWSTER COUNTY

We quit Fort Davis on a Friday morning. We packed it in and—after saying our goodbyes to the motel's staff, who seemed a little bewildered at our leaving—began the long drive south to Terlingua, a town that rests like a tattered blanket spread along the Texas border.

To reach Terlingua, we drove Highway 118 one last time. Past the World's Greatest Rest Stop, the wonderful Chihuahuan Desert Nature Center, inside Musquiz Canyon, through Alpine and past Sul Ross University we drove enveloped in a cool morning's embrace.

On the south side of Alpine, civilization takes an abrupt and permanent vacation. The eighty miles of desert and ranch land between Alpine and Terlingua are wondrous—so heaven-filled that the land itself could convert. The desert and mountains, impaled by the black knife of highway, are limitless both in their scope and ability to astound. The drive, as through any desert, can be very enjoyable if the car is worthy. If the car is shy or sickly, this is one of those tough roads that should be dreamed of and aspired to rather than attempted.

Sixty-five miles south of Alpine, we passed the Longhorn Ranch Motel and, from previous travels, knew that we were just twelve miles from Terlingua. At this distance, it is time to again observe speed limit signs, as the Highway and Border Patrols are usually lurking like turkey vultures.

I would write that we were getting close to the Terlingua town limit; however, there is no official boundary. Proudly unincorporated, you are either in town or you are not; you are never approaching the limit. The idea

The Waldron Quicksilver Mine, Terlingua. *Courtesy of the General Photo Collection, Archives Sul Ross University.*

of Terlingua is subjective. If you can see the village, or some part of it, then you have license to consider yourself there. Like so much of this part of Texas, being in Terlingua is as much about an actual presence as it is a state of mind. And that name, underlined red here on my computer due to its spelling, has as much mystery attached as does the name Marfa.

The name Terlingua means "three tongues" (languages) in Spanish, or so everyone seems to think. Everyone is convinced about the Dostoyevsky associations of Marfa, though, too. The area, evidently, takes its moniker from Terlingua Creek, which has run through the territory since forever. However, that still does not explain much; where did the creek derive *its* name? Clifford Casey, a local historian and an early professor at Sul Ross University, wrote:

> *When we check the official records of Brewster County, we find that for the first twenty or so years there was no definite agreement in the use of the name or names to designate the major creek now known as Terlingua Creek. In official records we find such terms as Tas Linguas, Las Lingas, Terlingo, Latis Lingua, Tres Lingas and Tres Linguas.*[35]

A few years ago, while writing another article about the place, I made a point of asking everyone who appeared to know what the three languages are that compose the name. Most frequently, I heard Spanish, English and

The Chisos
Mountains, early
morning.

Indian. Which Indian language, no one seemed to know. A few gave French
as the third language of the trinity. This trip, when someone gave the answer
of Spanish, American and Mexican, my wife laughed out loud. Again,
Casey commented:

> *There seems to be no end to the stories as to the origin of the name: three
> Indian tribes living up the creek—Apache, Comanche and Shawnee—each
> speaking a different language, Tres Linguas; three branches of the creek—
> Goat, Calamity and Crystal Creeks—or the three tongues of Terlingua
> Creek; three languages spoken in the area—Spanish, English and Indian.[36]*

There is also the story of an intoxicating drink made by the Indians from
a plant indigenous to the creek, the *Tezlingo* plant.

The name remains as much a mystery as the territory itself. The State
Historical Association recounts how

> *the original site was a Mexican village on Terlingua Creek three miles above
> the confluence with the Rio Grande. With the discovery of quicksilver in
> that area in the mid-1880s, the Marfa and Mariposa mining camp became
> known as Terlingua; the original site was then referred to as Terlingua
> Abaja, or lower Terlingua. When the Marfa and Mariposa mine closed in
> May 1910, the Terlingua post office, which had been established in 1899,
> was moved ten miles east to the Chisos Mining Company camp; the name
> was retained.[37]*

A miner at Waldron Quicksilver Mine, Terlingua, 1916. Most received one dollar per day. *Courtesy of the Smithers Collection, Archives of the Big Bend.*

Terlingua Abaja is now located within Big Bend National Park; it is, like so much associated with the region, a ruin. Nevertheless, it is a well-known bit of history that the Terlingua area was initially settled, in the 1880s, by miners and their employers after the discovery of quicksilver, or mercury, in the cinnabar ore. Indians had used the reddish paste for generations to illustrate both their bodies and the rock and cave wall canvases. And since, during the late nineteenth and early twentieth centuries, mercury was used in the fuses of bombs and bullets, mercury mining became a very lucrative industry for about the next fifty-five years, or until the end of World War II.

Today, the "ghost town" exhibits the mines and dwellings of all of those who lived and died in the area during this boom period. Visitors today can see several mobile homes and such placed within the adobe and brick shell ruins left from this era. Indeed, the famous Terlingua cemetery is the final resting place for dozens of members of this population, many of the grave markers dating back to the late nineteenth and early twentieth centuries. Obviously, exposure to the mercury was a cause of death for many of those in the cemetery. The influenza epidemic of 1918 was the cause of many of the others.

When the mercury mines were closed in the 1940s, those associated with the production moved on, leaving the region a ghost town in its most literal sense. The territory remained that way, desolate and lonely, for decades. Mainly those who wished to be away from the frenzy of civilization inhabited the town. However, in the 1960s and '70s, the area was rediscovered. The annual chili cook-off was established in the late 1960s and continues today on the first weekend of every November. This event, along with a few others, has brought the tourists to the area. This entire portion of the state, from Fort Stockton to the border, has seen a great resurgence in tourism. In fact, the chili cook-off is what first brought my wife and I back to the area years ago.

Ore cars from the quicksilver mine, Terlingua, Texas. *Courtesy of the General Photo Collection, Archives of the Big Bend.*

The motel my wife booked for us was located on Highway 170, the unofficial main street of the town. This is the road that runs westward to the resort town of Lajitas, with its grand hotel and golf courses, and eastward to Big Bend National Park. Luckily, the motel's management placed us alone in the back portion of the property. As such, we found ourselves relaxing in a room that seemed—and, if you think about it, was—just a box dropped into the middle of the desert.

Luckier still, every time that we travel to this part of the state, my wife excitedly and patiently waits for a glimpse of a roadrunner. We see them from time to time scurrying across the highway as we drive along, and each time my wife delights in their smooth, flightless speed. This afternoon, while we unpacked, one of these delightful birds decided to present itself as a sort of representative of the species and shuffled back and forth in the rocks and grass in front of our room. When he ran to the back of the building, we followed and saw that he was trying to find some shade under an abandoned truck. He seemed to know that it was waiting for him there. Never having been so close to one of these birds before, we were both surprised that it is a larger bird up close than from the window of a speeding car. They are not so much bird-sized as cat-sized.

In the heat of the afternoon and after a long desert drive, we poured ourselves into the motel's bed and listened only to the breeze flow across the landscape. There was no television, and the radio was able to receive only the distant, alien crackle of Mexican *cháchara*.

Terlingua cemetery. *Photo by Angie Browne.*

After waking, we sat outside on the porch in the red metal chairs provided. We could see, in the blue-gray, heat-clouded distance, the peaks and rolling terrain of Big Bend National Park. The wind brought the aroma of dust and heat. Relaxing in the late afternoon, we absorbed the immensity of the Chisos Mountains; the vista was punctuated by the twin-towered Mule Ear Peaks. This is a view that is obvious from just about every elevated position in the area and has been a landmark of the territory since the prehistoric oceans receded.

Every time that we have visited the area, we have always made time for a trip to the Starlight Theatre. This restaurant/bar at the back edge of the ghost town has been in operation since the very early twentieth century, when Howard Perry, the "King of Terlingua" and owner of a plat of land that held a rich quantity of cinnabar ore, built a church, a school and a theater for the miners, other employees and their families involved with the mining operations. The motel's manager told us that the theater offers a happy hour that includes dollar tacos and margaritas. We were going. But we were going to the ghost town not just for sustenance but also for a dose of attitude realignment that can only be administered by the staff on the "Porch."

The Porch outside of the Terlingua Trading Company—a general store of sorts (more souvenir kitsch than staples), replete with a one-room

The Terlingua Post Office. Today this area is the store and "Porch." The town is in the background. *Courtesy of the Smithers Collection, Archives of the Big Bend.*

museum—is as well known as any ranch or watering hole. The Porch extends about thirty yards, reaching from the front door of the store to the Starlight. It is a wooden plank bench, with the wall for backing—a communal arrangement, the old style—"neighbor-maker" seating. There are no partitions and no armrests. Every evening, the Porch fills with locals and tourists alike, each sharing their day's stories or general philosophies.

During our evening there, we met the British man who splits his time, paradoxically, between England in the winter and Terlingua in the summer. There was the young man with his guitar, girlfriend and songs who told us how they had just returned from Spain after being "chased all over the place by the Spanish police" for singing in the streets unlicensed. Then, of course, there is "Dr. Doug." Doug is as much a fixture on the Porch as the porch is a fixture on the Porch. In fact, Dr. Doug is the "borderline mental therapist" who offers his services from Dr. Doug's Mental Health Clinic—or, as his website states, "Guided Group Therapy on the Terlingua Ghost Town Porch."[38] Dr. Doug's therapy frequently involves "taking your medicine," and luckily, the Trading Company sells this prescription.

If you wait a few minutes on the Porch, inevitably a guitar will appear. Oftentimes a fiddle and a harmonica will join in. At that point, if not already uncased and tuned, beer will take a chair in the ensemble. After a few more minutes, even the most timid of the group will begin singing along while the Chisos Mountains recede into the dark ether on the far horizon. The dogs sit quietly, mostly, listening to the music and claiming an inability to read the sign above them: "No Dogs Allowed on Porch."

The Porch in full therapeutic swing.

My wife and I passed our night in Terlingua in this way, listening to songs and conversations alike, the one occurring in harmony with the other. While we sat and heard about the latest gossip, however, I was surprised to hear that "the ghost town has wi-fi now. The whole place is wired up." At first, I thought it was a joke. However, it seems that that Scylla "Progress" has pushed a toxic talon even into this far corner of demi-civilization, and when this occurs, that Gorgon sister "Development" cannot be far behind. Indeed, real estate prices and what parcels of land were "on the grid" or "off the grid" were common conversations that night.

To say that I was disappointed would be an understatement. At first, I felt horrified, violated. Now I have begun to accept the idea, as I would any bad news. However, just today I heard other, even more disturbing news. The Starlight Theatre, that icon of the Terlingua landscape, has closed indefinitely. I heard from an employee at La Kiva, another local watering hole and iconic settlement, that the plans are for the Starlight to see another opening in the near future. Hopefully, by the time this book reaches publication, the theater will have its characteristic Christmas lights restrung and relit. Hopefully the stage where countless musicians and others have performed, off and on, for near one hundred years will once again hold the weight of the traveling artists and their dusty equipment.

The good news is that the Porch is still open and that Dr. Doug's clinic is still offering its old-time therapy. Good thing. With the recent dusting of "Progress," there might be a wait to speak with the doctor.

We awoke with a desert's sun the next morning. It was not long before it shone white and hot, losing its cool, tawny morning's complexion. Out here, wasting no time, the sun goes straight to work.

As the light lifted the mountains again from the desert floor, we drove east, past Terlingua's sister community, Study Butte,[39] toward the Big Bend. Being so early in the day, I was worried that maybe the park was not open. After a

The Chisos Mountains
of Big Bend Park. The
Mule Ears Peaks are in the
background.

short fifteen-minute drive, we arrived at the park's entrance. Another couple
of minutes brought us to a ranger's checkpoint station. The sign in the station's
front window read that the fee was twenty dollars for a seven-day pass, and I
balked at entering. We were only going to stay for the day, we thought, so I did
not want to spend that much for the time we would be there.

My wife said, "Why not?" We were pulled over on the side of the park's
road, dickering back and forth on the merit of a twenty-dollar bill. The
entire time we spent on the roadside, we were only a few yards from the
ranger's station. I was sure that at any moment, the ranger would leave the
box and come over to ask us just what the heck we were up to. After debating
our money issue for a full five minutes (my wife's point, that we should just
pay the amount and enjoy our time in the park, of course carried the day),
I pulled up to the window of the checkpoint. There was no one inside.
The side window was closed, and a notice that we should pay the fee at the
nearest ranger station within the park was taped from inside. I apologized for
being a miser, laughed and rolled my eyes at the sky, at an entity that I felt
was probably doing the same in my direction.

Later that afternoon, we began our return trip home. Knowing very well
that the drive, even just back to the interstate, is exhausting, we stopped in
Terlingua for fuel, drinks and food.

There is a kind of freedom in beginning a journey from such a distant point—
freedom due to the absolute extreme position of the trip's inception. And for a
Texan, for whom a seven-hour, four-hundred-mile trip can be just an afternoon's
chore, even this reach from the border to Austin had the potential to be flagging.

At times, when standing outside in the Big Bend territory, the knowledge
of just how remote and alone you are induces a type of benign desperation,
a resignation to all that is larger and beyond yourself. To begin from
this vantage point is to have a clear track, to have all lanes open with no

competitors. Such was the origin of this final leg of our trip. There was the freedom to start this final heat with no other objective than simply to reach home, sometime. There could be no need for speed because the end was foregone and the journey was completed.

The route home that we chose was longer than the alternative. However, we retraced our steps through Fort Davis for no other reason than it offered greater viewing pleasure. We wanted, once again, to drive the paths of those earliest explorers and settlers. So, we drove up to Marathon and had another look at the historic Gage Hotel. We crossed the main street and found the old Marathon jail, hunched on the side of a side road in the old town, looking more like an old storage facility than jail. We stopped and had a look inside. The imposing and severe bars are still separating the anteroom from the cells in the back; a door of thick black bars was the entrance to the back rooms. There was evidence that in the recent past the jail had been open and used as a museum. An old mannequin stood at wilting attention in the corner, dressed in a standard-issue, black-and-white striped prisoner's uniform. A few pictures of past sheriffs that hung on the wall seemed placed as additions for the museum rather than remnants of what had hung there ordinarily. A few pieces of furniture appeared to date to the time when the jail was operational.

Down this same street we came upon that old cattle ramp that the ranchers had used to load their herds onto the trains for transport to market. The chute is overgrown with tall grass and weeds now, but the dark, wooden structure still protrudes through the detritus of the years and still serves as a very real, and even historic, reminder of that industry responsible for the initial settlement of Marathon back in the nineteenth century. I wanted to have a closer look at the old ramp; however, a worker was milling around

The old Marathon jail.

inside the old corral, and he and his dog were unsure about the strangers inspecting his work space.

We reached Alpine again after taking a left on Highway 90 at Marathon. Being the Sunday of the 2010 World Cup final game between Spain and the Netherlands, we had to find a spot to watch the game. Luckily, we found the perfect venue just across the highway from Sul Ross University, the Buffalo Rose. We had eaten at this restaurant once or twice on previous visits through the area, and as luck would have it, the bar in the back was almost empty, so we were able to ask permission to switch the channel to the Spanish television station to catch the game. A retired marine, a veteran of Vietnam, sat with us, and we three watched the game together. He told us that he had coached his grandson's soccer team in Alpine and that this activity, coupled with a few years in Germany with the Marine Corps, had piqued his interest in the sport. Fortunately, he was a Spain supporter, as were my wife and I, and soon he and I were yelling good-natured invective at the Netherlands team while simultaneously shouting encouragement to the Spanish from half a world away. Before long, a Hispanic man from the dining room came in, stood behind me and asked, "What's the score?"

"Still zero to zero," I replied, and after a glance to his wife, seated by herself now, he brought up a chair from a near table and joined us for a few minutes. Now the Spanish team had a small but strong fan base in the west Texas desert. "That Spanish goalie is really a remarkable young man!" the marine stated, and the rest of us eagerly agreed.

"What's the score?" a couple of cowboys at the bar wanted to know now.

"Still nothing, nothing," our marine answered, and the cowboys directed their attentions back to the beer in front of them.

With a Spanish victory secured, we headed back northwest, took a final lap through Fort Davis and enjoyed another turn up the Wild Rose Pass within Limpia Canyon. We noticed on this trip up the canyon trail that the fencing for the old Fort Davis remuda extends all the way to near Wild Rose Pass, a distance of a few miles from the fort. It was incredible to consider that the remuda would reach so far from the old fort, but the fact that it did only speaks to the importance and great necessity of the horse to these early settlers.

This trail, State Highway 17, intersects the interstate at the town of Balmorhea. It was here that we made our last stop before launching ourselves onto the interstate for that final push home.

During one of the evenings around the pool at the motel in Fort Davis, an Alpine native asked my wife and I what we planned to visit in the area. "If

The stone wall extending north from Fort Davis off Highway 17, a remnant of enclosure for horse remuda.

you see nothing else while you're here," he began, "you guys absolutely have to do two things. Number one, go to the observatory and experience a Star Party. Secondly, you *must* swim at the Balmorhea pool at the state park there. The place is just beautiful. You shouldn't miss it."

He had been so emphatic about visiting the place that I highlighted the item in my notebook since it was, of course, already penciled in. In fact, the very next afternoon we had begun to drive that direction when a very large thunderstorm swept in over Limpia Canyon. The thunder was magnificent, shaking car and ground alike. However, it was the massive bolts and flashes of lightning that finally deterred us from the pool. A visit was going to have to wait for safer weather.

On our way out of the canyon that last day, we did have better weather and arrived at the park about mid-afternoon.

Balmorhea State Park was established in the early 1930s, and the pool and nearby housing were built as part of Roosevelt's New Deal projects, with construction carried out by the Civilian Conservation Corps. In fact, the CCC is responsible for several projects in this part of the state—many of the buildings in the Big Bend Park, for instance. The park itself consists of 45.9 acres that includes San Solomon Courts, a motel built in the traditional Spanish Colonial architectural style so prevalent of the period and located just across the parking lot from the pool itself.

The pool, at 1.75 acres, is the highlight of the park. Reaching depths of twenty-five feet and a constant temperature of seventy-two to seventy-six degrees, the pool is a favorite destination for swimmers and

The entrance to Balmorhea State Park, Toyahvale, Texas.

scuba divers from across the country. As a swimming hole, the pool is unmatched in its uniqueness. In addition to the motel within walking distance of the pool's edge, there are also large changing rooms inside the gates and picnic areas just outside. Because the park is situated off the interstate and, technically, in the small village of Toyahvale, the pool and park alike are set apart from anything like it anywhere else in the state. In every respect this park is extraordinary. Indeed, at one end of the pool, near the diving boards, there is a fish conservation area cordoned off from the swimming public, and this spot has an underwater viewing area to allow for inspection of the animalia, as well as the deeper sections of the pool. However, the waters are used for more than recreation.

Driving around Toyahvale, one notices that the ditches along the road are actually trenches filled with cool fresh water. The farmers and ranchers of this area have been irrigating their lands for generations with the natural spring waters.

Before the settlers, the pool area was named Mescalero Springs for the Indians who inhabited the region. Today, the name "Balmorhea," as strange as it seems, is really just an amalgamation of the names of three of the area's developers: Balcome, Moore (or Morrow) and Rhea.[40] Remembering other names such as Murphyville, Marfa or Terlingua, Balmorhea does not seem so unusual after all.

On the afternoon we arrived at the park, the lot was full of campers, buses and cars. Local church and school groups had taken the day for a swim, too. In short, even for the middle of the week the place was busy.

As we entered the office, the young lady behind the counter held a phone in one hand and a walkie-talkie in the other. She appeared only slightly flustered by the exercise and gave us one of her available index fingers as indication that she would be with us in a minute. When she had hung up the phone, she directed "Ok. 10-4. Keep me posted on the car with the trailer" into the walkie-talkie. She turned her attention in our direction and seemed relieved to hear that we only wanted to take some pictures and walk around for a few minutes.

Once inside the pool area proper, my wife and I were amazed at the water's lucidity. Fish darted here and there around the feet and ankles of the children playing in the water. The line for the high dive was short but as constant as the squeals and yelps that accompanied each leap from the board.

The pool at Balmorhea. Fish conservancy and underwater viewing areas are just to the left of the splash impact.

The shallow end of the pool supported a few of the parents and other adults enjoying the sun and water from their floats. And even in the July heat, the water's temperature was cold to a first touch.

We were as reluctant to leave this park as we had been all of the others, but with a long, arduous drive before us, we took our final few photographs and loaded ourselves back into the car.

Balmorhea and Toyahvale are close enough to the interstate to hear the rumbling of the trucks and cars but distant enough to not see them. There is a sort of shroud barrier between this peaceful, beautiful section of the state and the more sterile, industrious workings of the interstate. Nevertheless, we parted company with this pastoral part of the state, and as we entered the on-ramp for the superhighway, both my wife and I fell silent. Each of us was experiencing a sense of loss, coupled with the memories of a wonderful adventure. Without a word spoken, we both knew that we would need to return soon, to experience again the history and myth that make up west Texas.

Note: The Starlight Theatre was reopened as of late November 2010. My wife and I had dinner there on December 4. The food and atmosphere were wonderful, as usual.

8.

Southern Brewster County

Big Bend National Park

The morning that we left Terlingua, we had headed straight for Big Bend National Park. The park was, in some regards, the focal point of our trip. After the aforementioned balking at the entrance, we proceeded on through the wilderness and the great expanse of the land. While there are many activities that one can enjoy while in the park, certainly one of its greatest pleasures is just driving through.

It is said that the Indians' story of the Big Bend's creation is that the "Great Creator," after forming the rest of the world, saw that he had several odds and ends of leftover material. In an effort to be rid of the detritus, he threw it all down in one area, and that spot is the Big Bend. It is as credible a theory as any. As far as the flora and fauna are concerned, the Big Bend is as diverse an area as any on the planet. The Chisos oak, for example, grows solely in this region; the same holds true for the Chisos agave. To try and make note of all of the rich and varied animal and plant life in this region is a herculean task left for the botanists and zoologists. However, there are an abundance of books, articles and dissertations that attempt just this labor. There is no denying the fact that the terrain of the Big Bend appears to be where the great whirlwind of nature first began its primordial gyrations and that this is the epicenter of that colossal chaos.

To describe the history of the park is a much lighter responsibility but one that still has multiple layers of development.

It is a well-known fact that early man inhabited this region, even back into the Paleo-Indian era or 10,500–6500 BC. There are several archaeological

Big Bend National Park. The southwest entrance is just past Study Butte.

sites in and around the park where study of early civilizations is ongoing. Not too long before then, the area was ocean. Marine fossils have been found high in the mountains, and much of the strange land formations are due to this event.

The Comanche and Apache Indians controlled the region for many, many generations. The Spanish explorers, though several traveled through the area, kept most of their focus on the coastal sections of the state—or those spots where the French were showing interest. As a result, the Indians kept the territory for themselves for much of early recorded history.

When the sections of the state from Fort Stockton to Terlingua were first witnessing settlements during the late nineteenth century, the Big Bend area did not get left behind—it only accepted civilization more reluctantly. In fact, the land has still not wholly acquiesced. There is an indomitable character here that resists all attempts of subjugation. The first generations of settlers out here came to understand that quality in the land and decided that instead of trying to harness the territory, they would try to preserve it as best they could.

A few ranchers have maintained a presence in the Big Bend region for generations. But it has been a hard existence. Life hangs from a thorny cord here. Cattle must be tended to judiciously in a land where rain is as scarce as the cool breezes that it brings. Illegal immigrants are routinely found, dead, in the desert, their empty plastic water jugs never too far away from the bodies. Paved roads and irrigation have mollified the desert to some extent, but there are still great stretches where even these technological advancements have little effect.

In some regard, the Great Depression is responsible for the creation of Big Bend National Park. In the earliest parts of the twentieth century, many attempts were made to grant Texas a national park. None was successful. Not until the 1930s did a serious inquiry into surveys and park standards develop when the issue arose concerning all of the employment that this work would generate within the state. United States senator Morris Sheppard is credited with delivering the idea to the director of the National Park Service, Horace Albright. Albright's reaction to a national park in Texas, while not cool, was not entirely warm, either. Albright wanted evidence that the region in question met certain criteria, most notably that the site should display "scenery of quality so unusual and impressive, or natural features so extraordinary as to possess national interest and importance as contradistinguished from merely local interest."[41]

For the next few years, support for the idea grew. Along with the urging of Texas congressman E.E. Townsend from Brewster County and Abilene representative R.M. Wagstaff, House Bill No. 771 was passed in the Texas legislature in 1933. This bill allowed for the creation of Texas Canyons State Park. Soon afterward, President Roosevelt approved the deployment of four CCC camps within Texas, one in southern Brewster County. The establishment of these construction camps all but assured Townsend, who had been pursuing the national park idea for years, of success for his efforts. New bills were introduced to the senate that enlarged the area of the park by several thousands of acres and changed the name to "Big Bend."

The Rio Grande at the mouth of Santa Helena Canyon.

The amount of acreage and the space needed to constitute a national park were tremendous. Big Bend State Park has a total of 160,000 acres, while Big Bend National Park is composed of just over 800,000. A large portion of these lands came from the so-called School Sections that the state of Texas already owned. Jameson wrote that "[i]n addition, tax delinquent lands in the area became eligible for park purposes."[42]

It is a sad fact that several families in the Big Bend area, already injured by the Depression, were more severely wounded by the passage of these bills that removed the one asset they had left, their land. Indeed, as the famous matriarch of the area, Hallie Stillwell, remarked about this period: "I was all for the park and I felt it needed to be shared with the world but I hated to see my friends, my ranch neighbors had to give up their homes. So, I have mixed feelings about that."[43] All in all, the state park saw its establishment in the mid-1930s, and the national park was finalized in the mid-1940s.

However, during the years leading up to the park's establishment, some saw not enough cause for such attention to the region. Some legislators argued that the Big Bend did not meet federal standards for national park status. Again, Jameson wrote that "[f]or some, Big Bend was the epitome of harsh mediocrity containing neither the highest peak in Texas nor gorges as deep as the Grand Canyon in Arizona."[44] The cause for such controversy was, of course, financial. There was always competition between states, and even between counties within individual states, for recognition of particular areas for those precious state and federal monies. Then there is the tourism aspect that the proper moniker will bring, augmenting a region's stature with a legal title.

My wife and I drove for some miles before coming to a fork in the road. Because neither one of us had ever seen the large canyons within the park, we decided that we would take the Santa Helena Canyon road. We drove the park's thirty-five-mile-per-hour speed limit for several miles. Because of the ascending and descending of the two-lane blacktop across the mountains and hills, traveling any quicker would have been foolish. Besides, we passed more than one bicyclist that morning—each was impossible to see ahead due to the rises in the road.

We reached Santa Helena Canyon in about forty-five minutes. The drive down into the canyon had seemed long, but the vistas were incredible. Now we parked the car near a picnic table and wondered where the canyon was located; we could neither see the walls of the canyon from the road nor hear the rushing of the Rio Grande from behind the bushes and trees beside us. We did take notice of the sign near the table warning visitors to take care of their foodstuffs because of the javelina in the area. The sign had a drawing of a snarling boar, and just this image was enough to set my wife's imagination going.

After we got our bag ready with camera, water and notebooks, we began the trail where it was marked and found that the ground—because it soon became soft, fine-grained sand—had a walkway made of narrow wooden planks roped together and extending almost all the way from the road to the river's edge.

When we came over a small ridge, the canyon lay directly before us, the Rio Grande rolling and curving. The vertical walls of the canyon shot straight up to the heavens, a rise of more than 1,600 feet from the river's level. To suggest that the sight awed us would do no justice to either the geography or ourselves. There are times when the magnitude of nature is so incredible, so beyond imagination or expectation, that expression is futile. This was one of those times. Because we stood at the edge of the canyon, we had sight of both the open Mexican land just across the river and the gaping, folding mouth of Santa Helena Canyon. We had arrived just as a canoe was heading into the darker portion of the river, inside the canyon walls. As the craft took its tack away from us, the speck of it in contrast against the titanic rock face, I felt small and strangely relieved of immediate responsibilities. The enormity of the landscape denied the importance of any man-made problems or drama. I was transfixed to that spot on the shore watching the raft float off around the bend. Soon, my wife stepped up beside me, and we stood that way, hands together and staring into the canyon's gigantic yawning mouth.

Later, we searched the shoreline for fossils and those smooth, color-filled rocks that are produced only by the rages of large rivers and oceans. I launched many of these over to Mexico, making illegals of them all. Some I submerged into the vacuum of international waters.

I had wanted to strip down and swim over to the other side for a moment. My wife even encouraged me to follow through with the insanity. However, I couldn't tell if the river was two feet deep or twenty nor where the rocks were. The waters were roiled by the current's rapid movement and appeared faster up close than it had seemed from the wooden walkway.

We spent about an hour walking up and down the shore and being envious of the rafters. We had the whole morning there to ourselves; no one else ventured up the entire time we stayed. It was just as well, because we were completely entranced by the beauty and spectacle of the place. And when it was time to head out, we walked away with a heavy foot.

Santa Helena Canyon, one of the "must see" items for any trip here.

Back at the car, nothing had been ravaged by a javelina. The only change in the landscape was the arrival of a park maintenance worker in his truck. He was eating his lunch.

The drive out of the canyon was even more relaxed than the ride down had been. We were familiar now, in a sense, and could take our time, knowing how far we were from the connecting road and, from there, Study Butte. Several times we parked the car just off the road—which is to say that we put the car in park wherever we felt like stopping—to take photographs of the strange foliage. My favorite Big Bend plant is the agave plant, also known as the "Century Plant." Despite the name, the tall stalk with its distinctive, semicircular, yellow/orange flowering, blooms at the end of a twenty-five-year cycle and then dies. This plant is all over the region but typically grows singularly and spaced far apart. Without a doubt it resembles a plant or tree from a Dr. Seuss book. My wife's favorite plant—from that one trip anyway; her preference changes with each visit—was the ocotillo. This is a towering, multi-armed spindle-like green plant that many mistake for a cactus. Due to the rains, these plants were blooming with ferocity. The great juxtaposition of the tall green stalks with the pinkish, red blooms is extraordinary.

We drove out of the park and back onto Highway 118. While we were refueling and stocking up in Terlingua, we both began to mentally retrace our trip. There is, for the both of us, a sense of loss and regret in leaving. We talk, as we always do when visiting someplace we grow attached to, of living in the region. The both of us have always held Terlingua close in our collective consciousness; however, I am afraid we could not endure the isolation for long.

Driving along 118, we passed a sign for the Longhorn Ranch Motel. The sign is, most likely, older than I am. It is sun-blanched and faded almost to the point of invisibility. It is the perfect example of the past receding into distant memory. There is evidence of this everywhere I look. While we drive, the countryside recalls all of those stories that we have read and heard during our time out here in the desert—many of them violent, some profane, others heartwarming. Whatever the tale, all have been impressive and have left their stamp on our souls. There is nothing so common as to be forgotten out here. Even the drawl of everyday life leaves its memory. Everything out here is extraordinary. Everything out here creates history. Everything out here becomes mythology.

During the entire trip, I was constantly looking for some emblem of the past I had been reading about: the gunfights, the insane personalities and the larger-than-life individuals who shaped an entire state and, in some regards, the whole nation. I kept a vigilant eye for signs of these things, because I was sure that somewhere someone had forgotten to take that sign down. Somewhere progress had missed that one icon of the past, and that one piece of history would connect the present with the recent past. I kept thinking

The ocotillo plant. Due to the rains, this plant was in abundance.

that we are not so far removed from those first settlers—maybe a generation or two but still within touching distance.

And then I had it. I thought of my father and how he would have been all of twelve years old when the park was signed into law in 1944. He always liked to say that, as a boy, he had seen Roosevelt in Houston in that famous convertible, smoking his long-filtered cigarette. If my dad was right, he would have seen the president at just about the same time as the park bill was signed. The more I thought on this, the more the past swam toward me. Men who had spoken with the early settlers in their old age wrote many of the books I read on the subject. These authors then passed away when I was young. And in there, in that cycle of life, I felt I had my connection to these wonderful characters, my connection to that fascinating history. In a way, we could all reach one another.

We drove home, burning across the interstate, and packed in the back were those items we had accrued in the desert: a few books, a couple of pamphlets, a poster, some rocks from the shore of the Rio Grande and a bucket of peaches from the tree behind the motel that had been so teeming with fruit it was pulling the tree down. But the greatest souvenirs are the memories and stories here.

We are driving 118 back toward town. I break a long silence by asking, "It's wonderful out here, isn't it?" My wife, without taking her eyes off the countryside, answers, "*Claro.*" Certainly is. Her gaze out of the car's window draws the silence back. After a few moments, still watching the landscape glide past, she asks, "When can we come back?"

Appendix

Maps

The following are useful maps for understanding the region and routes taken throughout this book.

Western Half of Texas. George F. Cram, geographer, engraver and publisher. Chicago, Illinois. *Courtesy of the Map Collection, Archives of the Big Bend, Sul Ross University.*

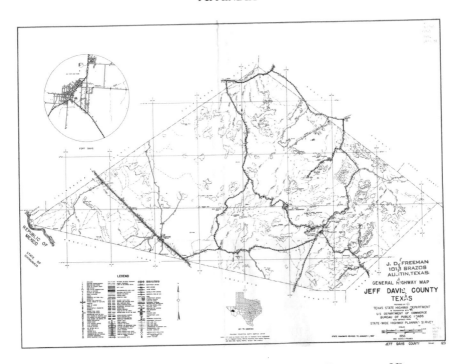

General Highway Map, Jeff Davis County, Texas. Texas State Highway Department. J.D.
Freeman. *Courtesy of the Map Collection, Archives of the Big Bend, Sul Ross University.*

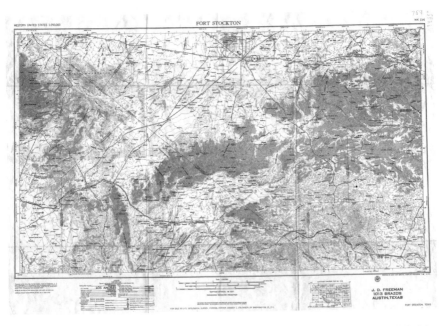

Fort Stockton, Texas. Army Map Service, Corps of Engineers. J.D. Freeman. *Courtesy of the Map
Collection, Archives of the Big Bend, Sul Ross University.*

Maps

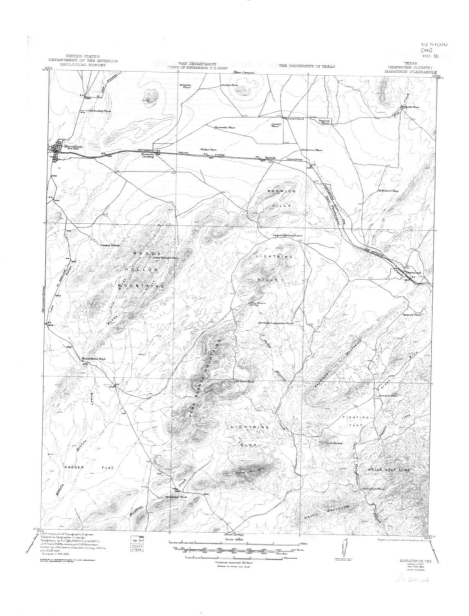

Texas, Brewster County, Marathon Quadrangle. United States Department of the Interior Geological Survey. War Department, Corps of Engineers, U.S. Army and University of Texas. C.H. Birdseye, chief topographic engineer. 1921 edition. Reprinted 1949. *Courtesy of the Map Collection, Archives of the Big Bend, Sul Ross University.*

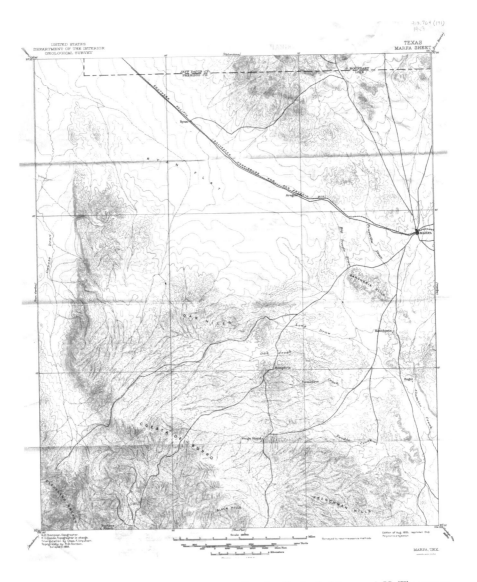

Marfa, Texas. United States Department of the Interior Geological Survey. A.H. Thompson, geographer. J.D. Freeman. 1895 edition. Reprinted 1949. *Courtesy of the Map Collection, Archives of the Big Bend, Sul Ross University.*

Maps

Texas, Terlingua Quadrangle. United States Department of the Interior and University of Texas Geological Survey. E.M. Douglas, geographer in charge. 1904 edition. Reprinted 1951. *Courtesy of the Map Collection, Archives of the Big Bend, Sul Ross University.*

Notes

Chapter 1

1. Lucy Miller Jacobson and Mildred Bloys Nored, *Jeff Davis County, Texas*, 1st ed. (Fort Davis, TX: Fort Davis Historical Society, 1993), 9.
2. Ibid., 41.
3. Barry Scobee, *The Story of Fort Davis: Jeff Davis County and the Davis Mountains* (Fort Davis, TX: Fort Davis Historical Society, 2004), 15.
4. Robert M. Utley, "A History of Fort Davis," ParkNet, 2002, http://www.nps.gov/history/history/online_books/hh/38/hh38m.htm.
5. Barry Scobee, *Nick Mersfelder: A Remarkable Man* (Fort Davis, TX: Fort Davis Historical Society, 1969), 5.
6. Ibid., 37.

Chapter 2

7. Clifford B. Casey, *Mirages, Mysteries and Reality. Brewster County, Texas, the Big Bend of the Rio Grande* (Seagraves, TX: Pioneer Book Publishers, 1972, second printing 1974), 103.
8. National Park Service, U.S. Department of the Interior, "The Original Settlers of Big Bend," www.nps.gov/bibe/historyculture/original_settlers.htm.
9. Ken Hudnall and Sharon Hudnall, *Spirits on the Border V: The History and Mystery of the Lone Star State* (El Paso, TX: Omega Press, 2005), 85.
10. Hallie Stillwell in *Recollections of a Pioneer: A Documentary Short by Derek Carroll*, Javelina Waltz, Austin, Texas, 2008.

Chapter 3

11. Eddie Cope, the TXGenWeb Project, Anna Stella Frazier "Annie Riggs," http://www.rootsweb.ancestry.com/~txpecos2/annie-riggs.html.
12. Robert K. DeArment, *Twelve Forgotten Gunfighters of the Old West*, vol. 1 (Norman: University of Oklahoma Press, 2003).
13. Ibid., 143.
14. Ibid., 149.
15. Glenn Justice, "Comanche Springs," TSHA Online: A Digital Gateway to Texas History, Texas State Historical Association, 2010, www.tshaonline.org/handbook/online/articles/CC/rpc3.html.

Chapter 4

16. Sul Ross State University, "A History of Sul Ross," www.sulross.edu/pages/3718.asp.
17. Sul Ross State Teachers College Bulletin 20, no. 4, "Course Work Leading to Bachelors' And Masters' Degrees" (1939).
18. Clifford Casey, *Alpine, Texas: Then and Now* (Seagraves, TX: Pioneer Book Publishers, 1981), 21.
19. Ibid., 143–48.
20. Barry Scobee, *The Steer Branded Murder* (Fort Davis, TX: Fort Davis Historical Society, 1952, republished 2004).
21. Ibid., 11.

Chapter 5

22. J. Frank Dobie, "The Writer and His Region," Sul Ross State College Bulletin 33, no. 2 (1953). West Texas Historical and Scientific Society Publication.
23. The Big Apple, "Marfa (summary)," http://www.barrypopik.com/index.php/new_york_city/entry/marfa_summary.
24. Texas Escapes, "Texas Museums," http://www.texasescapes.com/Texas_architecture/TexasMuseums.htm.
25. Lee Bennett, "Fort D.A. Russell," TSHA Online: A Digital Gateway to Texas History, Texas State Historical Association, www.tshaonline.org/handbook/online/articles/FF/qbf14.html.

Chapter 6

26. Otto Struve, *Publications of the Astronomical Society of the Pacific* 55, no. 324 (June 1943): 124. W.J. McDonald Observatory of the University of Texas, http://articles.adsabs.harvard.edu/full/1943PASP...55..123S.

27. Dr. David S. Evans, "McDonald Observatory," in *Jeff Davis County, Texas* (Fort Davis, TX: Fort Davis Historical Society, 1993), 279.

28. Harlan J. Smith, "50 Years of McDonald Observatory: Frontiers of Stellar Evolution," McDonald Observatory ASP Conference Series, vol. 20, edited by David Lambert (1991), 3.

29. Evans, "McDonald Observatory," 280.

30. Smith, "50 Years of McDonald Observatory," 12.

31. Hobby-Eberly Telescope, http://www.as.utexas.edu/mcdonald/het/het.html.

32. Struve, *Publications of the Astronomical Society*, 129.

33. Texas Parks and Wildlife Department, "Indian Lodge," www.tpwd.state.tx.us/spdest/findadest/parks/indian_lodge.

34. Chihuahuan Desert Nature Center, http://cdri.org.

Chapter 7

35. Casey, *Mirages, Mysteries and Reality*, 142.

36. Ibid.

37. Texas State Historical Association, http://207.58.4/handbook/online/articles/TT/hnt13.html.

38. Douglas Blackmon, Dr. Doug's Mental Health Clinic, http://www.drdougs.com/On-the-Porch.html.

39. The community was named for William Study, a manager of the Big Bend Quicksilver Mine in the early twentieth century.

40. John Troesser, ed., "Balmorhea, Texas," Texas Escapes, http://www.texasescapes.com/TOWNS/BalmorheaWestTexas/BalmorheaTexas.htm.

Chapter 8

41. Horace M. Albright to Vance Prather, February 3, 1931, File o-32, Part I, BBNP, RG 79, NA in John R. Jameson, *Southwestern Studies: Big Bend National Park—The Formative Years* (El Paso: Texas Western Press, University of Texas at El Paso, 1980), 6.

42. Jameson, *Southwestern Studies: Big Bend National Park*, 9.

43. Stillwell, *Recollections of a Pioneer*.

44. John R. Jameson, *The Story of the Big Bend National Park* (Austin: University of Texas Press, 1996), 26.

Index

A

Alpine 20, 34, 36, 68, 70, 78, 82, 84,
    89, 113, 124
Arnarsson, Ingólfur 105

B

Balmorhea 20, 65, 134, 135
Beltran, Bernardino 21
Big Bend National Park 9, 41, 127,
    138, 141
Buffalo Soldiers 25

C

Casey, Clifford 34, 79, 125
Chadborn, Daniel 58
Chihuahuan Desert Nature Center
    121, 124
Chinati Foundation 102, 106
Chisos Mining 126
Civilian Conservation Corps 120, 135

D

Davis, Jefferson 24
Davis Mountains State Park 120
Dobie, J. Frank 86
Dostoyevsky, Fyodor 90

Dr. Doug 130
Duforat, Jean-Michel 11, 50

E

Emory, William, Major 24
Espejo, Don Antonio 9, 21

F

Flavin, Dan 104
Fort D.A. Russell 103
Fort Davis 9, 14, 20, 22, 28, 36, 56, 61,
    68, 72, 87, 102, 112, 115, 124
Fort Stockton 14, 15, 18, 50, 54, 56,
    59, 62, 65, 70, 128

G

Gage, Alfred 39, 40
Gage Hotel 36, 38, 133
Gallagher, Peter 62

I

Indian Lodge 120, 121

J

Johnson, Lyndon B. 15
Judd, Donald 103, 104
Junction, Texas 16, 18

INDEX

K

Kabakov, Ilya 104
Kokernot Springs 79

L

Lajitas 128
La Kiva 131
La Linda Bridge 41, 47

M

Marathon 13, 34, 41, 133
Marathon jail 133
Marfa 20, 34, 69, 79, 89, 98, 102, 110, 125
Marfa Lights 110, 111
McDonald Observatory 113, 114
McIvor, Violet Locke 115
Mersfelder, Nick 30
Mescalero Apaches 9, 24
Murphy, Thomas O. 79
Murphyville 79, 89, 136
Museum of the Big Bend 77, 79, 85
Musquiz Canyon 36, 71, 124
Mùsquiz, Manuel 36

O

Overland Trail Museum 27

P

Paisano Hotel 93
Paisano Pete 55
Patton, Nan 43
Pecos County Jail 63
Perry, Howard 129
Potter, Walter 43
Powe, H.H. 80
Prada Marfa 109, 110
Presidio County Courthouse 92

Q

quicksilver 35, 126, 127

R

Riggs, Annie 55, 56
Riggs, Barney 57
Rodriguez, Fray Augustin 21
Roosevelt, Franklin D. 120, 135

S

Santa Helena 141
scenic loop (Highway 166) 69, 121
Scobee, Barry 24, 30, 31, 80, 85
Smith, Harlan 113, 119
Southern Pacific Railroad 34, 79
Starlight Theatre 129, 131
Star Party 116
Ste. Genevieve winery 11, 50, 119
Stillwell, Hallie 40, 43, 86, 141
Stillwell, John 46
Stillwell, Roy 43
Stockton, Robert F. 62
Struve, Otto 113, 114
Study Butte 131, 144
Sul Ross University 70, 74, 125, 134

T

Terlingua 11, 44, 70, 82, 124, 127, 136, 139
Terlingua Creek 125
Townsend, E.E. 140
Toyahvale 136
Trost and Trost 39, 95

V

Valentine, Texas 32, 107, 108, 109
Verne, Jules 90

W

West Texas Historical and Scientific Society 78, 85
Wild Rose Pass 20, 22, 134

About the Author

Courtesy of Lee Miller.

Byron Browne writes a monthly column for the online magazine *Texas Escapes*. In addition, he has written extensively on topics ranging from the bullfights in Andalusia to Texas wines. He lives in Austin, Texas, with his wife, Angie.

Visit us at

www.historypress.net